D0934220

Life on the Wing

Derwent May
Life on the Wing

A Bird Chronicle from the pages of *The Times*

Illustrated by Peter Brown

The Robson Press

First published in Great Britain in 2012 by
The Robson Press (an imprint of Biteback Publishing Ltd)
Westminster Tower
3 Albert Embankment
London SE1 7SP
Copyright © Derwent May 2012

ISBN 978-1-84954-249-4

10 9 8 7 6 5 4 3 2 1

A CIP catalogue record for this book is available from the
British Library.

Set in Adobe Garamond Pro and Penmanship Birds by Namkwan Cho
Cover design by Namkwan Cho

Printed and bound in Great Britain by
CPI Group (UK) Ltd, Croydon CR0 4YY

Contents

Acknowledgements

Many thanks to the editor of The Times _for permission to use material from my weekly 'Feather Reports'._

Introduction

On the January day when I began to write this introduction to my book, a song thrush was singing for the first time this year in the trees at the end of my garden. The notes rang out loud and clear – bright, crystal-clear notes and trills, now repeated three times, now four, on and on in the morning sunlight.

Every year, for several years in the past, there had been a song thrush singing there from January to June. Then, in the last two years, none came, and there was silence in the treetops. It was exquisitely pleasurable to think that once again – throughout the spring, with luck – I was to have that song, itself so joyous-sounding, just outside my window.

That intense pleasure in birds began, I think, on country walks with my father and sister when she and I were small children. Then, when I was fourteen, I set out to study the willow warblers that came in summer to a birch common near our home – plotting their territories, finding their nests, watching them bring up their young. I had written two articles about them in bird journals – *British Birds* and *Ibis* – before I left school.

Then other interests in my life supervened. But in due course I started taking my own son for long walks in the countryside – along the Ridgeway and the Malverns, and in the Lake District – and suddenly all my delight in birds flooded back. I think it got a special boost when I met an elderly ornithologist who addressed me: 'Ah! Willow warbler May!'

For thirty years now I have been writing about them in *The Times*. I have followed their lives in many regular haunts of mine – estuaries, marshes, heaths, the seashore, as well as countless woods and fields and country lanes. I have also sought them in wild places, in mountains and on islands.

But I can find pleasure in them anywhere. Even a starling flying past my window – a few flaps of its wings, a glide, another few flaps, in its inimitable way – can give me, for a moment, all the contentment that I wish for.

Derwent May

January

In the churchyard of St Mary's, in the village of Bayford in Hertfordshire, lies the body of one of the greatest British ornithologists, William Yarrell. His authoritative book, *A History of British Birds*, was published in 1843. It was illustrated by 550 engravings and it became an immediate bestseller.

The pied wagtail was given its scientific name in honour of Yarrell – *Motacilla alba yarrellii* – and the French, touchingly, still call the pied wagtail the *bergeronnette de Yarrell*, or Yarrell's little shepherdess.

He has a fascinating tomb in the hillside churchyard, with its views to the north across the blue countryside. A broken railing overgrown with nettles surrounds it, and inside are the graves of his whole family. He died in 1856, and wrote his own epitaph for the tomb: 'He was the survivor of 12 brothers and sisters who, with their father and mother, are all placed close to this spot, first and last. The earliest summoned and the longest spared are here deposited.' You can still see all their tombstones: long stone casings on the ground for the adults; little stone plaques for the children.

While I was looking at the tomb some goldfinches were making their tinkling twitters at the top of a bare ash tree and a robin was singing softly in a hedge. The churchyard also had several neat yew trees, and suddenly a redwing flew out of one of them. No doubt it had been feeding on the juicy, pink yew berries.

Redwing

It was followed rapidly by another, then another, and suddenly the whole sky to the north of the churchyard was filled with redwings flying about in their wild, erratic way. The sun was low in the sky behind me but its rays were strong and fell directly on the flying birds. So the bright red feathers under the wings of these wintering thrushes all shone out brilliantly as the flock whirled around above the sunlit landscape.

It was a spectacular sight while it lasted. I could not help feeling that Yarrell must have seen it sometimes in the winter, and that he would have been glad to know that the birds were still performing above his tomb, more than 150 years after he died.

Four blackbirds have been coming on to the lawn in my garden to eat the food that I have been throwing down for them.

One is a handsome male, jet black with a bright yellow bill and a yellow ring round his eye that gives him a wide-eyed, startled look. Another is an adult female, with very consistent dark-brown plumage except for some paler feathers under her chin. Then there are two younger birds: a young, black male that can be distinguished by the dark-brown ends of his wings and his duller yellow beak, and what I suppose is a young female, brown with a very mottled breast like swirling muddy water.

I think they are a family from last summer, though there is no evident family feeling between them. In fact, watching their relationships is very interesting. If the adult male comes down first, he seems to regard himself as owner of the garden, and flies fiercely at the next comer. The intended victim generally dodges him and stays, and the others follow it down. After that the 'owner' shows no interest in the other birds until they come near him.

However, if the adult female lands on the lawn first, she seems to take the view of herself that the adult male did of himself and moreover he now seems to share that view. I see him sitting on the fence looking down at her very warily – and, sure enough, as soon as he drops down onto the lawn she flies at him. She is now the 'owner'.

Nevertheless, before long they are all feeding in the garden together again. They tuck in eagerly but repeatedly pause to look round the garden and up at the sky for fear of enemies.

The young ones are less aggressive, but they too will sometimes try to chase another of the party away. In fact, between them, they spend a lot of time quarrelling and leaving the food unattended. A song thrush comes down occasionally, and once I saw the adult female fly at it, and land at the end of the garden. The thrush just flew nimbly over her head, picked up the very crumb she had been eating and fled with it. The blackbird's attack had just been self-harming.

Why do blackbirds behave like this? In the short term it

clearly does them no good. The answer must be that in the long term their aggressiveness serves them, and that all in all they live better the more aggressive they are. Still, you often feel like shouting at one of them: 'Stop it, you idiot!'

Last week I went in search of a flock of waxwings. These birds, the size of starlings, that have come here from Scandinavia have provided an extraordinary Christmas treat, not only for birdwatchers, but also for many others who have seen them in high streets, car parks and gardens. They have swept down from Scotland and spread all over the country looking for berries to feed on and have found them on ornamental bushes such as cotoneasters in the centre of numerous towns and villages.

I found my flock in a crescent of new houses on the edge of Hertford. There was a field just behind the houses and there, in the tops of some tall, young sycamores, there were forty-five of them (they were easy to count) silhou-etted against the sky. Their swept-back crests, like tiny sails, identified them at once, and the frayed tips of the crests looked like the bunches of thin seed stalks that were dangling from the sycamore twigs around them.

They held their wings out from their sides like a penguin's flippers, as if poised to fly. From where they sat they had a clear view of an ornamental rowan tree, loaded with pink and white berries, in one of the gardens.

Waxwing

Suddenly, about half of them shot down into this tree. There they swung about among the berries, gobbling them in an almost manic fashion. Now I could see all their colour – the pink of their bodies and crests; the black and white markings; the blob of red, like sealing wax, on their wings; and the bright yellow tips to their tails. They stayed in the tree for no more than twenty or thirty seconds. Then they all rushed back to the sycamores like a shoal of startled fish.

It was a marvellous spectacle, and during the next half-hour it was repeated again and again – the wild dash into the tree, the acrobatics and frenzied gobbling, then the coordinated, desperate-looking flight back.

Then, in a single motion, the whole flock rose into the

air and whirled away through the sky. If I had arrived half an hour later, I would never have seen them.

I was walking past a grove of willow trees at the edge of a lake when I heard a faint, strange squeak up in the branches. I was not sure what it could be and I searched the twigs with my field glasses, but there seemed to be absolutely nothing there. Then I heard it again and realised it was just one willow branch rubbing against another in the wind – not a bird at all. It was not the first time I had been caught out by a tree in this way.

However, in the silence of a winter's day one can often detect thin, puzzling sounds, hard to locate, in the trees – and some of them do come from birds.

A little further on I again heard some slight murmurs. Once again I lifted my field glasses and this time, perched on top of a tall hawthorn bush some distance away, I saw a goldfinch, with its red, white and black head.

As I got nearer, more wispy sounds came from inside the bush. As my goldfinch took off, another three goldfinches suddenly darted out of the bush to join it. They were evidently the performers, if the word is not too grand. Now, as they all swung away, I could see the long gold bars running down the length of their wings to the tip.

A flock of goldfinches is called a 'charm' and it was the right word for this dazzling little band of tricksters. Girls seeing that sight overhead were once supposed to be sure of getting a rich husband.

Another bird that can sometimes be heard only faintly in the treetops is the siskin. It is a small, green bird with a yellow wing bar and there can sometimes be a whole flock of them extricating the seeds from the black cones on an alder tree, with only the slightest, occasional wheezes and tinkles coming down from it.

They are hard to see, too, as they hang among all the cones and catkins that festoon the alder twigs. You could easily pass under the tree without realising they were there at all. 'Siskin', their sibilant name, is itself an imitation of their calls. They are relatives of the goldfinches and the two species might be called the whispering birds of winter.

The other day I passed a large stretch of grass that ran down to a river, with the sun breaking through the clouds after a morning of heavy rain. The grass was wet and all the earthworms beneath must have come to the surface, for there were birds pulling them out everywhere – blackbirds, several magpies, a song thrush and even a crowd of moorhens.

Suddenly down flew a small flock of thrush-like birds that skittered to a landing and instantly joined in the feast. They were redwings – winter visitors from Iceland and Scandinavia. They are quite like the song thrush, but unmistakable with their yellowish eye-stripes and the big splash of blood red on their flanks.

But very soon something startled them and up they all flew to reveal that the blood-red patch extended right under their wings as well. They looked like the flying wounded as they shot into the sky, tilting wildly from side to side.

No doubt they fly in this erratic way to protect themselves from cruising peregrine falcons and sparrowhawks. In fact, a few years ago I saw a remarkable battle between a redwing and a sparrowhawk.

I heard a shrill cry of fear coming from a hawthorn bush and in it I saw a dark-brown female sparrowhawk spreadeagled among the thorns. Beneath her, upside down, was a redwing, the crimson blaze showing under an outspread wing.

Both were completely entangled in the thorns. The sparrowhawk was holding the redwing lightly with one of its talons, unable to wrench itself free without letting its prey go; the redwing was completely trapped. Total deadlock. The situation was resolved only when a man with a dog came by and the sparrowhawk gave up and tore itself away. The redwing flew off ruffled but unhurt. It had no doubt tried to save itself by diving into the hawthorn – and succeeded.

Redwings are widespread in winter. They will be going home in April, and between now and then flocks of them will be singing in the treetops. You hear the distant murmur, and then find them sitting among the branches babbling away.

The earliest spring visitor here is the chiffchaff, and sometimes in March I have heard one of these new arrivals singing in the treetops, with the redwings performing alongside it – the voices of winter and spring ringing out together.

Since *British Birds* magazine began in 1907, it has presided over a colossal expansion of interest and pleasure in birds in this country. Countless birdwatchers have published their field observations in its pages – but always subject to the most careful editorial scrutiny of their accuracy and scientific soundness. It has been the school of British birdwatching.

There is a typical and topical letter in the current issue. In autumn 2004, there was an invasion of northern bullfinches. These birds, which come from Russia and Finland, are slightly bigger and brighter than our bullfinches, yet not very easy to distinguish. However, it seemed to be the case that they had a distinctive call – a tooting or trumpeting note. Nevertheless, many observers thought that they also made the soft, piping 'peu' call that our bullfinches use. If so, it was never going to be so simple to pick them out.

In a letter, James McCallum reports from a visit to Finnish Lapland in spring 2006, where he found that all the breeding northern bullfinches used the trumpeting call and no other. He had also watched a female northern bullfinch among some British bullfinches in Norfolk in March of that year, and again observed that the northern bird always used the trumpeting call and the British birds the 'peu' call.

He says that it may have been easy to think mistakenly that the northern bird used the soft call. When he came along a path where the little flock were feeding on old blackberries in the brambles, he could hear both calls ahead of him. But the shy British birds melted away invisibly into the leaves, leaving only the northern bird conspicuously behind. So an observer may well think that this bird had been responsible for making both calls.

He also mentions a loud, clear, flute-like song he heard from the northern birds, again quite unlike the British bullfinch's subdued – and rarely heard – song. It made me remember how some twenty years ago I found a male bullfinch looking very colourful on top of a hawthorn tree near Windsor and carolling away loudly in a startling and totally unfamiliar way. I now wonder if in those days, before anyone had ever thought about them, I had found a northern bullfinch. Well, it is the moment for bird-watchers to go out, armed with better information, and see if there is another invasion – which is quite possible if the weather turns cold.

Dippers are getting busy. These birds of upland burns and streams are among the first to nest and can have eggs in their homes behind waterfalls by the end of February.

The rushing water they live by will not freeze; they retreat to lowland canals only in the most terrible of winters.

They are a remarkable sight as they bob up and down, blinking, on a rock in the stream before dropping into the water and disappearing. They spend much of their life walking about on the stream bed, looking for little aquatic creatures. They also swim underwater, although they do not have webbed feet, instead using their stubby, well-feathered wings.

On the rocks their cocked tails make them look like large, white-breasted wrens; for this reason they have always been considered close to the wren in the evolution-ary tree. However, ornithologists now think that this is a bit naive and that, in fact, they are close to thrushes.

They are singing again after two quiet months – a sweet trilling song, not unlike a wren's – and the males and females, which split up last summer and held rival territories next to each other along the stream, are joining up once more.

Like kingfishers, they are often seen shooting past you just above the water. I have watched them on a burn in the Lammermuir Hills and noticed how, fast though they may be going, they always stop at the same point. That is where the next territory begins and they respect the boundary. They drop down on to a stone, or start flying back, so you need not fear that you have lost them. If you follow them, you will almost certainly meet them again. Few birds are so obliging.

Even when the water is icy, dippers will plunge in, and the young birds are as fearless as their parents. On the same burn I once watched a very young bird, a small, drab version of its parents. It gave me one look from its rock before leaping into the water. I never saw it again, but I'm sure that it went sailing off happily down there.

People often use the phrase 'lesser spotted' by way of a joke. The *Daily Mail* once called Prince William's then-fiancée 'the lesser spotted Kate', because no one ever saw her, and in *The Times* Ann Treneman described our former Prime Minister as 'the lesser spotted Gordo' for the same reason. It all goes back to a tiny and not very common bird: the lesser spotted woodpecker.

Lesser Spotted Woodpecker

It gets its name because there is a great spotted woodpecker, which is large with white spots on its back, and 'lesser spotted' follows naturally for the smaller, similar species. However the 'spotted' is not so apt here because the small bird has black and white bars on its back, rather than spots. I have seen a similar bird in America, which is called the ladder-backed woodpecker, and that would be a better name if it were not already taken.

This is the best time of year to go looking for the lesser spotted woodpecker, which is an elusive bird. It is less than six inches long and, when it is searching for insects in tangled treetops, it is hard to see. However, at the end of January it starts to be very audible. It drums with its beak on dead branches, and it also makes a sharp 'pee-pee-pee' call.

Both of the spotted woodpeckers drum, in order to attract a mate and warn off rivals. It is a loud sound that rings through the woods. However, one can sometimes distinguish the lesser bird's drumming, because it is thinner and more high-pitched, and each burst goes on longer than the great's, which lasts only about one second.

The 'pee-pee-pee' call is only heard for a few weeks around February. It is not unlike the nuthatch's call and if you try to see every nuthatch you hear, you may well find that you have a lesser spotted in the tree. The bars on its back distinguish it from the great spotted, which also has a big blood-red splash under the tail that the lesser spotted lacks. Look out for this sprightly little bird not only in woods, but also in copses and even solitary trees in hedgerows.

February

One evening I was walking in the London dusk alongside the Thames and, just as I passed the back door of the Savoy Hotel, I was arrested by a burst of fluting song. The singer was hidden somewhere in the dark trees in the little garden flanking the river, but it could easily see me, I have no doubt, because of the many-coloured lights from the river. It was my first singing blackbird of the year, making the most of the nocturnal light of London.

It is always a marvellous moment when you hear that first blackbird. Its song is so beautiful and you know that from now on you will hear more and more blackbirds singing, until the summer evenings are filled with lazy music. The rich notes seem to fall effortlessly from their open beaks and float away, curling into the air. Occasionally, the singer seems bored with it all and his song collapses into a jumble of thin, hard notes. But it is only for a moment – and then the gorgeously indolent fluting begins again.

Blackbirds are now the birds people probably see most often in their gardens, especially the males, conspicuous with their sleek, black plumage and their bright yellow beak. Both the male and the brown female, moreover, are very active birds, hopping boldly over lawns and chasing off other blackbirds.

We are lucky here, because until the nineteenth century they were much more exclusively woodland birds. In fact, that low-pitched song evolved because it was better at penetrating a dense canopy than a high-pitched song would have been. It is both far-carrying and soft. By contrast, when blackbirds are alarmed they fly off with a shrill, clattering cry, theatrically hyping up the panic, I feel.

They are mostly in pairs by now, and in April they will start building their nests in garden hedges as well as in odd sites such as the glove pocket of an abandoned car. People often give names to their garden blackbirds. I recently heard of one called Nigella, partly after the nyjer seeds that birds love in bird feeders and partly after Nigella Lawson.

Even while there has been frost in the air, magpies have started building their nests for spring. This week I watched one in some bushes pulling clumsily at the twigs. It kept tumbling about, and now you could see how useful its long tail was. In the sky, where it looks like a saucepan handle, the tail seems nothing but an encumbrance. But in the bushes, spread out and gleaming, it helped the bird to keep its balance in the most efficient way.

Eventually the magpie managed to break off a long twig, cackled loudly and flew off with it. It is the males that collect building material, and this one's mate had been sitting nearby watching. She flew off with him, and somewhere away in a treetop they would have helped each other to weave it into the nest. Some of last year's constructions can still be seen in the bare trees, often battered and ghostly looking. But magpies normally make a new nest each year, and it is desirable for them to start early, since the bulky structures take a long time to finish.

Of course, many people will groan at the very thought of magpies breeding and multiplying, since they fear for the day in spring when they have some young robins in a nest in their garden and wake up to find the nest empty and a magpie laughing on the roof. But the magpie is behaving no differently from the robin when it pulls up an earthworm to give to its fledglings, and the idea that magpies seriously reduce the number of small songbirds has now been proved false.

I continue to like magpies and the bold way in which they perch on treetops, like the flag-bearers of the countryside. Incidentally, in some international bird lists they are now called black-billed magpies. An accurate description – but I don't believe anyone in this country is ever going to adopt that alien name, whether they love or hate the bird.

One morning I was out in my garden just after sunrise looking at a song thrush which had already been singing for hours in a sycamore tree. The sun's rays had just caught its breast and it was looking almost pink.

Song Thrush

Then I noticed two larger pink birds sitting in a tree nearby. They were two jays, but they were sitting as close to each other as two turtle doves. They were both preening a lot and shivering their wings. It was, I think, too early in the year for them to be getting down to the business of mating and breeding, but there was certainly a spring air of intimacy about them.

The thrush and the jays were the only birds about and a line of Shakespeare came into my head. Autolycus's cheerful song 'When daffodils begin to peer' in *The Winter's Tale* includes the passage: 'The lark, that tirra-lyra chants, / With heigh! with heigh! the thrush and the jay.'

I had never thought before about this odd linking together of the thrush and the jay, or if I had, I had supposed that 'jay' was only there for the rhyme (further on, with 'hay'). But suddenly I wondered if Shakespeare had not seen a thrush singing and some jays flirting at the same time, just as I was seeing them now, with my daffodils also 'peering', just about to open.

This pair of jays had spent the winter together, I believe, for since last autumn I have often seen a pair around the garden. Jackdaws, which belong to the same family as jays, the crow family, are starting to sit side by side in pairs in the same cosy-looking way, but I had not seen jays sitting like this before.

What will be seen in the next month or so is small flocks of jays gathering in trees, and then flying out, with one trooping after the other to another tree. Magpies, also members of the crow family, gather in the same way in early spring, but much more conspicuously, with a lot of loud chattering. When there are twelve magpies in a bare tree, all pointing their long tails in different directions, it looks like a giant pincushion.

Both the magpie and the jay flocks appear to be made up of first-year birds that have not got a mate yet, and are now in the process of forming pairs. Valentine's Day is the day on which birds are traditionally said to pair up.

Blackbirds, dunnocks and greenfinches all start singing in early February, but, for me, the chaffinch really signals the onset of spring. This week, a little later than in some years, they, too, have been joining the party. And with them there it really does sound like a party.

They have one of the most cheerful-sounding of all British bird songs. It begins with a little run of chirpy notes, then the notes come louder and faster, and finally it breaks into a whirl that sounds as if the bird has turned head over heels. They repeat the song again and again. In the nineteenth century people gambled over which of their caged chaffinches would sing the most songs in a set period of time.

Chaffinches also look very fine as they sing, and as they generally perform on a low branch and are not very shy, it is easy to watch them. It is the males that sing, and they are now in their spring plumage with a powder blue cap, a pink breast, a greenish lower back and two conspicuous white wing bars. These males have now taken up their territories and they are flying around the boundaries making loud 'pink-pink' calls, so that other chaffinches know precisely the limits they must not cross. Only the brown female chaffinches are allowed in, and when the male has chosen one the pair will defend the territory together. After that, another distinctive call, like a rapid trickle of water, will be heard everywhere. Nobody knows what its purpose is, but it may be a warning of danger from the male to the female, or perhaps a call to let her know where he is.

With all this vocalising, chaffinches become a noticeable presence in the countryside from now until July. They build their mossy nests in April and bring up about four chicks. There are getting on for seven million pairs in Britain, which means that they are probably our second most common breeding bird after the wren.

A very strange-looking goose is slowly becoming more widespread in Britain. It is a large, pinkish bird that looks as if it has two black eyes, and when it flies it reveals large white patches on its wings. In the water it swims gawkily with its tail held higher than its shoulders, and it can be seen perching in trees. This curious creature is the Egyptian goose, a common bird in Africa. In Kenya, there is one on practically every village puddle.

It was introduced here in the late eighteenth century and Norfolk has always been its headquarters in this country. It is most abundant in Holkham Park and along the Babingley river. But it has been spreading into the East Midlands and is now not uncommon further afield. It is mostly seen around lakes and gravel pits, and there was a pair on the Round Pond in Kensington Gardens recently.

Altogether there are thought to be about 1,000 individuals here, all living wild and flying freely. It is on the British list in the C category, which is defined as 'established feral birds that are self-maintaining' – the same category as the ring-necked parakeet. ('Feral' in this context means non-native birds that live freely here.)

At this time of year they are particularly noticeable, since they nest early, and the ganders are fierce defenders of their territories. Two ganders will face each other, flapping their wings and trying to bite each other at the base of their long necks, as well as scrabbling at each other with their feet. They will also try to chase away other intruders, and in Kenya there are records of them successfully driving off crocodiles. They nest in holes in trees, and lay clutches of eight or nine eggs.

However, they have not got a reputation for much success as breeders. Canada geese harass them, carrion crows eat their eggs, and because they nest so early it often means that the eggs or young do not survive because of the cold. This year, if the weather continues as it is, they may do better.

Canada geese – which are in the same category as the Egyptians, though they are far more numerous – are also getting excited this month. The breeding pairs are flying around together with wild yodelling cries and the ganders will soon be courting their mates with 'triumph displays'. They run at a nearby male with their neck stretched out and chase it off, then return to their mate proudly with loud, crowing cries. Sometimes they will do this when there is not even another gander there. But the female seems just as welcoming.

At Amwell gravel pit in the Lea Valley, north of London, I saw quite a rare bird – a little bunting. There is a large reed bed there on one side of the flooded pit and a swathe has been cut through it, leaving just a floor of dead reeds. Several species of bird regularly come down to feed in this swathe, especially reed buntings and chaffinches. Besides natural seeds and insects, they can sometimes find seeds there that have been scattered especially for them.

Little buntings breed in northern Finland and in the taiga

further east, and migrate south in the autumn, with a few of them drifting across to Britain in most winters. As a rule, it is only resolute seekers who have seen them here. But one had been reported intermittently in the swathe since the end of January, and when I arrived I found the familiar army of birders lined up behind a fence, peering down hopefully at the reed floor through their tripod telescopes.

The little rarity had been seen about an hour earlier, but had not returned. However, it was a pleasant enough scene for the patient watchers, of whom I now became one. Reed buntings were constantly coming down, including some handsome males already sporting their black head, white collar and white moustache.

There were also streaky-brown female reed buntings, who were quite hard to pick out on the reed litter, as were the brown female chaffinches. Dunnocks crept out of the reeds. Now and then the little flock would suddenly fly up, alarmed by something unidentifiable, but they would soon be back.

An unexpected thrill were two water rails who kept coming out of the reeds and stalking about – beautiful, rarely seen birds, with long red bills and finely barred blue underparts. Out on the water, a great black-backed gull loomed over two lesser black-backs and two snow-white smews were diving earnestly in the distance. Lapwings flew overhead.

But what we were waiting for was a bird very like the female reed buntings, only smaller and with redder cheeks. Suddenly the cry went up, 'There it is!', and I caught a brief glimpse before it immediately flew back into the reeds. We continued to wait, until finally, after another hour, it came back and settled down at the edge of the swathe. It crouched close to the ground without moving and we were all rewarded for our patience with a clear view of its chestnut-red cheeks glowing in the sun. A modest trophy – but it was agreeable to think that we had seen such an uncommon visitor from so far away.

Bittern

Bitterns are beginning to boom. These herons of the reed beds make an extraordinary, explosive sound that can be heard three miles away. It is like their spring song. It used to be believed that they produced this noise by blowing down a reed, but now it is thought that a sudden expulsion of air from their chest sets their thick windpipe vibrating. The great booming sounds once gave them a reputation as magic birds. More materially, they were served at royal banquets and considered good eating.

What still makes them mysterious is that it is so hard to see them in the reed beds. Bitterns are naturally camouflaged, with long black, brown and yellow streaks that blend in with the reeds, and they increase the effect by pointing their necks and long, sharp beaks at the sky.

I have watched one at Cheshunt, in the Lee Valley, north of London. Having, with great difficulty, detected it standing among the reeds, I found that if I took my eye off it for a moment I immediately lost it again. In the end I identified a dried-up nettle in the reeds near its head and was able to navigate my way back to the bird via this, its outline and then the rest of it miraculously gleaming forth again. What can help locate them sometimes is that they produce a blue powder to clean their feathers of slime from the eels that they eat, which can give their whole plumage a bluish tinge.

In 1997 these birds were very rare, with only eleven bitterns known to be in Britain, most of them in East Anglia. Since then, under the auspices of the Royal Society for the Protection of Birds (RSPB), many acres of new reed beds have been planted to encourage them, and by

2011 there were nearly a hundred. They are more common in winter, with birds flying in from the Netherlands, and during cold spells they are seen in reed beds across the south of England, often in quite small ones. When the lakes are frozen they even come out and parade on the ice, looking very gawky and uncomfortable.

Lapwings are returning to the fields where the wheat and barley are coming up in low, green lines. The males come first and are just starting to display in the air. These superb black-and-white plovers are establishing their territories and trying to attract a mate.

They have two flight displays, which I watch every year over a large sloping field – one whole side of a valley – in the Chiltern Hills. At first, the bird goes zigzagging round his territory, rocking from side to side and showing alternately the black upper and the gleaming white underside of his round, floppy wings. It is like a light show in the sky.

Then he goes on to his second display – if this does not frighten off his rivals and attract a female lapwing, then nothing will. He flies up higher, crying 'pee-wit' (another name for the lapwing). When he reaches the top of his climb, he turns, calls again, and with a particularly loud 'pee-er-wit' comes diving down, twisting and turning crazily as he drops.

He may repeat these two displays several times before he lands. You can hear the 'pee-wit' call from a long way off, and I have often hurried to see one displaying.

Lapwing

When a female who has tracked down the male lands in his territory, he approaches and performs a ground display for her. He shows her his black breast-band and scrapes the ground with his feet, as if he were preparing a nest. He tilts forward as he does this and lifts his tail, waggling it about so that she sees in turn his white rump and the bright orange underside of the tail. She may be unimpressed and fly away. But if she likes him, she will stay and will probably become his mate. Female birds of most species are particular about whom they choose for a mate.

Lapwings are not really black. At closer quarters you can see that they gleam with a wonderful green and purple sheen. The brilliance of a male's plumage and the vigour of his displays are what count with females, and research indicates that a particularly fine male may end up with two females in his territory for the rest of the summer.

March

L ast week I explored a new estuary for its birds – the Thames estuary. A friend had recommended the shore at East Tilbury, a few miles below the Tilbury docks, and we made our way there together, past the Victorian sea defences of Coalhouse Fort, through some scrub, to the edge of the beach. The tide was well out, though coming in, and a broad stretch of sand lay before us.

The first birds we noticed were the dunlins all over the sand. They looked at first glance like little stitches in a smooth canvas. But they were not motionless stitches – there were hundreds of them all running about, some in the middle of the beach, some further out where the small waves were breaking.

Scattered among them there was quite a number of larger waders, rather hunchbacked and moving about less. On the Essex estuaries further north I have often seen large flocks of golden plovers, but these were a less common species: the grey plover. Grey plovers are often solitary birds, and these all seemed independent of each other, though there must have been a good hundred of them out there. In summer they have beautiful silver and black plumage; these were in their grey winter feathers, but it was a delicately mottled, silvery grey, and they remained handsome birds. From time to time we heard their mournful triple cry, and when they flew up it was easy to see their distinctive black 'armpit' and the white bar along their wings.

Other birds along the shore were shelducks, some piping oystercatchers, one or two solemn-looking curlews and a knot of common gulls. But what we were hoping for were avocets – and soon we saw them. A flock of about thirty of these lovely birds, snowy-white with fine black markings, came flying up-river and settled at the edge of the water, where they pranced about on their long, blue legs. We walked along to the seawall, from which we saw another, larger flock. Then more and more flocks came flying in, no doubt disturbed by the incoming tide, and spread themselves along the shore.

Suddenly, they all went up in the air together – at least 700 of them – and flew round and round over the water. It was an extraordinary sight. As they all twisted and turned, flashing alternately black and white, they were like a rippling aerial reflection of the waves below them. Finally, a large flock settled on the water, where they became almost invisible. I had never seen so many avocets together. It seemed unbelievable that these were rare birds in Britain fifty years ago.

Herons are nesting and I went to look at the heronry in Regent's Park, London. The herons first arrived there in 1968 and now there are more than twenty gigantic nests in treetops on the islands in the lake. In the bright morning sunshine I had a wonderful view of some of these from across the water, as I stood on the bank below the bandstand.

Heron

There were four nests in one tree alone and others dotted about in trees around. The branches beneath the main tree were white and ghostly, where the guano of many seasons had fallen on them. The whole scene was curiously peaceful, with one or sometimes two herons standing motionless on every nest. They made a striking tableau with their sleek black and grey bodies, their black crowns and crests and their long, yellow beaks, now flushed with red at the base.

The herons have been building up their nests of stout twigs since February, and have reached the moment when they are beginning to mate. But for most of the day there is little to do, so if they are not off fishing they merely stand very still by their beds, as it were. Occasionally one left the roost, stretching out its long neck as it took off, before resting its head between its shoulders again as it flew away. One or two others arrived, weaving their way through the branches before coming down on the edge of their nest. Once, a bird that was already there lifted its beak and touched the beak of the new arrival.

Then I saw what I had been hoping to see – a pair mating on the nest. The two birds were standing side by side and suddenly one of them crouched, while the other, obviously the male, climbed up onto its back. Then there came a spectacular moment. The male lifted its wings and, without flapping them, held them in a V-shape like a great, silky-grey canopy above him and his partner. He looked as enormous in this posture as any bird in Britain could ever look. As he came down, the female put up her beak and touched his just as the other one had done. It seemed a gentle beginning to what would be a busy family summer.

Over towns as well as in the countryside, you can see a small bird flying quite high in an extraordinary way. It is beating its wings slowly, rocking from side to side and weaving a very erratic path through the sky. It is also singing a fruity, rollicking song. When it lands in a treetop, you can see quite clearly that it is a male green-finch – apple-green, with a gold bar on its wing and a stout beak.

In the tree it may continue singing and might also make a loud wheezing note. This very distinctive sound can remind one of the 'cheese' in the yellowhammer's 'A little bit of bread and no cheese' song, but it is far more emphatic and pungent – more like a loud, sucking kiss.

The display flight, the song and the wheezing are all ways in which the cock greenfinch advertises its pres-ence to possible mates and rivals. An odd feature is that while most male birds sing and perform in, or directly above, their territory, the greenfinch, which has quite a small territory around the bush it nests in, goes ranging far and wide in its song flight. It has been suggested that although the bird is warning other males not to come too close to its little territory, it is also, paradoxically, trying to attract them. This is because greenfinches nest in loose colonies, not too far from each other, and this benefits them when they go searching for food together. So their aerial performances may serve to invite other greenfinches to join the colony. One should never underestimate the subtlety and complexity of bird behaviour.

Greenfinch

Unfortunately, greenfinches have been suffering lately from a disease called trichomonosis. This makes it impossible for infected birds to swallow, so they starve. Last year they were wheezing healthily all over London and in the countryside around, though they had diminished in numbers in some other parts of Britain; this year, sadly, I have not heard so many. However, chaffinches were also seriously affected a few years ago and now appear to be flourishing again. It must give one hope that the greenfinches will also recover from this apparently rather fickle disease.

Reed buntings are singing again – and when they are doing so they are one of the easiest birds in the world to see. They like to perch right on top of the tallest reed in a reed bed, and if there is an even taller bulrush growing among the reeds they will sit on that. The males, who are the singers, have also just come into their spring plumage. They look very dressed-up, with their jet-black heads and bibs, white moustaches and a white collar, while the rich chestnut and black patterning on their back is like a Turkish rug.

The song, however, I am sorry to say, is not much good. It consists of only a few wheezy or scratchy notes. If you transcribe it into English words, it sounds something like 'My, my! What a swizz!' This is repeated again and again, and can get very monotonous as you sit in a hide waiting for a bittern, say, to show itself among the reeds. It is sung quite quickly when the bird is using it to get a mate. But once he has a female in his territory it slows down, as if there is no need to make the effort any more. The females are easily distinguished because they are brown where the males are black, but they have the white moustaches and a pale collar.

These buntings are relatives of the yellowhammer, or yellow bunting, and in recent years many of them have left the reed beds to join the yellowhammers in the fields. In their traditional watery haunts they nest in bushes among the reeds, but out in farmland they often make their nests in oilseed rape. The males sing, just as conspicuously, on top of the rape plants. The yellowhammers stay in the hedges.

One bit of behaviour for which reed buntings are famous is feigning injury. Like partridges and ringed plovers, both of which are also well known for this trick, buntings will try to lure predators away from their young by pretending that a wing is broken. I have sometimes followed one down a boardwalk in a marsh as it scrambled along, trailing a wing most pathetically. I was not deceived – but foxes often are. Once it feels its brood is safe enough, the fraudster bunting flies swiftly up and away.

I have just seen a small group of house sparrows in Trinity House gardens beside the Tower of London, and also one chirping loudly from a tree in a garden in Kentish Town, north-west London, where I have never seen one before.

Two sparrows do not make a revival, but perhaps there is a chance that they are coming back to the capital. Even after most of them disappeared from London, a small colony remained in London Zoo, and they are still there in the zoo's Gorilla Kingdom, where ten new nesting boxes have been put up for them. Perhaps recent London sightings are of birds that have started their lives there.

Forty years ago there were probably twelve million house sparrows in Britain. Now there are less than half that number, and city dwellers seeing them exclaim, 'Look – there's a sparrow!' – something they would never have done before. However, they are still quite common outside towns. I know plenty of hedges and bushes in villages around the country where I could almost guarantee to show you some chattering and chirping.

I have spoken to many ornithologists about these birds and it is clear that still no one knows why they have left the cities. Fewer insects for their young, fewer loose tiles and cracks in walls to provide them with nesting places, fewer of them in the countryside so that dwindling town populations have not been replenished – all these are plausible suggestions.

Where house sparrows are still found, they are very noisy at this time of year. The cock sparrow has no real song, but he sits above his intended nest hole making very loud single chirps. House sparrows breed in close colonies and do not hold large individual territories, but they protect their nest sites determinedly from other sparrows that would like to seize them.

An interesting thing that one often sees is a small flock of cock sparrows surrounding a female, chirping and seeming to peck at her underside. It produces quite a storm in a bush, until suddenly they all fly away. But what they are up to is not entirely clear. Probably one of them has started courting a female and the others have flown down and joined in.

The outburst does not normally end in any of the males mating with the female; however, one feels it must be some kind of display of prowess by the males, and perhaps leads to some future, more discreet conquest by one of them. Another sparrow mystery waiting to be solved.

The first chiffchaffs are arriving. This is around the traditional date for them, though in some recent years they have appeared much earlier. They are obviously a little hardier than the other warblers that visit us for the summer, which are generally April arrivals. The chiffchaffs also spend the winter further north, mainly around the Mediterranean, with quite a few actually staying in Britain for the season; the other warblers mostly go to hotter parts of Africa.

I have twice heard my first singing chiffchaff of the year in the first week of March at Maastricht, in the south of the Netherlands, when I was visiting the annual art fair there. It is always a great moment when you catch the first sound of their 'chiff, chaff' song ticking away in a treetop. They sing as they search restlessly for food through the branches – feeding up after their journey and announcing that they are back in their territory at the same time.

Through the field glasses, you can see that they are little birds with greenish-brown backs and faintly yellow underparts. They have black legs – this is one of the best ways of distinguishing them from the very similar willow warbler, which will also be back in Britain quite soon. Another method of telling the two apart is by their songs: the willow warbler has a much more beautiful song, a trickling cadence of descending notes.

Recently it has been realised that two subspecies of chiffchaff also visit us, mainly during the winter, with some still around at this time of year. These are the northern, or Scandinavian, chiffchaff and the Siberian chiffchaff. They are not easy to distinguish from our chiffchaffs, and twitchers have been having a hard but exciting time trying to identify them – especially as some individuals seem to be half way between the two in their plumage.

Broadly speaking, however, one can say that the Scandinavian chiffchaff is a little larger than ours, greyer above and whiter below; otherwise the two are very alike. The Siberian chiffchaff is about the same size as our bird, though it is said to look rather bull-necked. It lacks the greenish and yellowish shades, and in general has a sandy look. It also has a different song, more like a willow warbler's, and a different call note. Our bird makes a loud 'hweet', very frequently used and familiar to most birdwatchers, whereas the Siberian bird has a mournful, bullfinch-like call, appropriate, perhaps, to its melancholy homeland!

I have been in a remote part of Windsor Great Park that is like an ancient oak forest. Most of the oaks were planted under Queen Victoria's auspices around 1866, as a worn white plaque informed me, and they are very tall now, with long, writhing branches like Medusa's hair.

I used to know this forest well when I was younger and there have been two changes there since then. First, there is now a herd of red deer that wanders about and this has left no vegetation under the trees apart from bracken – dead and brown at present. So nearly all the birds are birds of the trees. Second, the most conspicuous of those birds is the ring-necked parakeet, the colourful alien that is colonising southern England.

The parakeets that day were, or seemed to be, everywhere. I say 'seemed to be' because they are very fast, noisy flyers, so they are like those garrisons in besieged cities that ran from one cannon to another to suggest that there were more of them than there actually were. The parakeets kept speeding from treetop to treetop like sharp, thin arrows with long shafts, screaming as they went – an amazing spectacle. And once, when I was standing on a mound, I had an unusual view of a low-flying pair from above. In the bright sunlight, their whole upper side was a marvellous emerald green. When they landed in a tree I could discern the red ring round the male's nape and their crimson beaks.

Ring-Necked Parakeet

Not everyone likes their presence here, as they are thought to be depriving great spotted woodpeckers of their holes. However, the other notable sound in the trees of Windsor Great Park was the drumming of great spotted woodpeckers. Parakeets or not, the great spotteds are increasing, not decreasing.

The other plentiful birds were jackdaws, passing in chacking flotillas, and in the bracken a few wrens were singing. A treecreeper was climbing up an oak trunk. Its streaky back blended with the bark, but as it leant to one side or the other its silvery underside gleamed out.

The wild geese are getting restless. Some of them have already begun their spring journey northward, and the rest are getting ready to go. There are pink-footed geese from Scotland and the sugar-beet fields around the Wash; white-fronted geese from English estuaries and the Hebrides; brent geese from the south and east coasts of England. They will all be off in their skeins, high in the sky, honking, yapping and laughing.

However, of all the geese that visit us for the winter, the one I find most delightful is the barnacle goose. It is a relatively small goose, with a beautiful, barred bluish-grey back, bright white underparts and what looks like a black stocking over its head and neck, with a hole where its white cheeks show through.

In Britain it is found mainly in the Hebrides – especially on the island of Islay, where I have spent many hours watching them, and in the Solway Firth. On Islay it shares the fields with white-fronted geese, but whereas the white-fronts stay near the ditches tearing up the grass, the barnacles are mostly seen a little higher up in the middle of the fields, nipping the grass with their dainty beaks. They murmur as they feed, and when they fly in flocks down to the sea lochs they make a sound like small dogs barking. These barnacle geese from Islay go back to nest in Greenland.

They get their name, it seems, because they were once thought to begin life not as eggs but as actual barnacles in the sea. There is a barnacle known as the goose barnacle because it is attached to the seabed by a long, rubbery stalk and the whole creature looks very like a goose's head and neck. It was from these crustaceans that the geese were thought to spring, because their nests and eggs were never seen here. So the barnacle ended up being named after a goose, and the goose ended up being named after a barnacle.

Actually, the young barnacle geese do have a remarkable beginning, though of a very different kind. Back in Greenland, the geese often nest on high ledges on the basalt rocks, in order to protect themselves from Arctic foxes. When the tiny goslings hatch, the only way that they can get down is by jumping – and jump they do, often falling hundreds of feet to the scree below and then having to slide down further. But in their downy coats many bounce up unharmed and complete their first, hair-raising journey in life successfully.

April

Wrens are moving up in the world. As the male birds extend their territories and hope to get mates, they start singing on walls and the higher branches of trees to make their presence felt. Their rapid, throbbing song no longer comes from under a heap of old, broken, orange bracken. As they hurtle their song out, one can easily watch their little brown bodies vibrating on these new, exalted perches. Sometimes two of them will have a song duel, facing each other across the border between their territories, and sometimes there will be an actual fight. Humans are ignored when they are quarrelling.

These male wrens are also busy in another way. They are building nests in their territory. They may construct five or six of their little domed grass nests in various holes and crevices, or in the heather on moorland. The idea is to attract females with them. If a female comes into the territory, the male will fly around showing her the nests. Should she decide to adopt one as her home, she will become the male's mate.

But the male wren does not stop at one mate if he can help it. He will go on showing visiting females around the nests, which are called cock's nests, and may end up with as many as three or four mates. However, he will show them very little attention after he has finished mating with them.

Each female will line her nest with feathers and make it suitable for the young, before laying six or seven tiny white eggs with red spots on them. She will also be mainly responsible for feeding the young birds, but the male may come and give her a little help, especially when the young are first fledged. There is some dispute over how much assistance the male offers at this stage.

A line of young wrens following each other through a hedge, their tails all cocked, with a scolding parent nearby, is one of the fine summer sights.

After this, the females themselves may move off and find a different male for another brood. So there is a good deal of swapping of partners all through the summer – fidelity is not important it seems for these minuscule birds.

Altogether, there are more than eight million wren territories in Britain over the summer. This could mean that, with adults and young combined, even allowing for heavy mortality, there might be more than sixty million wrens in the countryside at some moments during the year. That is as many wrens as human beings. It is a cheering thought.

I walked over the chalky hillside fields of Hertfordshire looking for three kinds of bird – corn buntings, yellow-hammers and linnets. The sun was strong and warm, the barley fields were green, the oilseed rape was turning yellow and the sky was full of singing skylarks.

I turned along a hedge in a valley between two fields where I have seen all these birds before, but on this spring day almost the first birds I saw were winter visitors. The sloping field on the far side of the hedge had been newly ploughed and the furrows were full of fieldfares. They looked almost as fat as partridges. It did not take them long to see me, and soon the air was full of them making their clucking cries and speeding off – seventy or eighty of them altogether. By now they may be on their way to Scandinavia.

I was disappointed not to see a yellowhammer straight away, but I went on, stopping occasionally to look at the blackthorn flowers, and suddenly I did hear a corn bunting singing. Or was it? Was I perhaps turning a snatch of skylark song into the song I wanted to hear?

But the corn bunting's song is pretty distinctive,

with its stuttering first notes and tinny little jangle, and within a few minutes I was proved right. It was clearly coming from the hedge, and as I approached stealthily I saw the corn bunting through a gap in the foliage, perched in a small tree on the other side. The plump, brown bird opened its beak in what looked like a snarl and sang once more. Then it flew off. It was the only one I saw that day, but at least I had found one of my birds.

I had to go a good deal further before I saw a yellowhammer. I heard its sharp 'click' call and there it was, sitting on top of a hawthorn bush, its head a wonderfully bright yellow. But I did not hear a yellowhammer's song.

I was on my way home before I saw a linnet. I was coming back beside the ploughed field when I heard the unmistakable twanging note, and five of them dropped down, two females settling on an old rape stalk and the others on the earth. Two of these were males with fine red chests. The males had a brief skirmish in the air, spreading their tails so that the white edges expanded to look like a white fan. Then, suddenly, there was a female yellowhammer on a ridge beside them, obviously attracted by all this activity.

A moment later they had all gone – but I had fulfilled my hopes for the day.

Meadow pipits are easy to recognise in the winter, but now that the first tree pipits are arriving from Africa, problems may arise.

The meadow pipit is a little streaky-brown bird with a longish tail that spends most of its time on the ground. But in spite of their name they are not really birds of the fields. In the breeding season they like heaths and moors, and the dunes along the coast, and at this time of year they are just beginning to nest under rough grass and heather.

They are practically unmistakable when they take flight. They go up as if they were climbing stairs, fluttering straight along, then climbing a little, and doing the same thing several times until they are as high as they want to go. As they fly, they make a very weak, peeping note two or three times. In fact, the German name for them is *pieper*. All in all they have a rather feeble appearance in the air.

Tree pipits are slightly bigger birds, mainly seen on woodland edges or in open country with plenty of scattered trees. However, they often come down to the ground – like the meadow pipit, this is where they nest – and then it can sometimes be quite hard to know which species you are looking at. The main differences are that tree pipits are rather more sleek and upright in stance, and look more yellowish on the breast. They also have pinker legs and a pale eye-ring.

The two species have similar song flights over their territories in spring. They both fly up, spread their tail and wings, dangle their legs and then parachute dramatically down again with their wings lifted and their tail closed. However, the meadow pipit usually goes up from the ground and returns to it, while the tree pipit flies up from a treetop or a prominent branch and then comes back to it, or settles on another nearby perch.

The songs they sing while in flight are quite distinct, however. The meadow pipit's song, as the singer rises and descends, is a string of thin, sharp notes – now faster, now slower – ending with a little trill. The tree pipit's song is similar in structure but far louder and bolder, and it ends with some strong, sweet, melodious notes as the bird lands.

It is easier, perhaps, to admire the elegant tree pipit. But I like the meadow pipit. It is a very companionable bird when you are out walking for hours on the moors or mountains.

Grasshopper warblers are arriving back from West Africa. They get their name not from any tendency to leap about, but from their song, which is somewhat like a grasshopper's fiddle music. Other comparisons have been to the sustained winding of an angler's reel – their singing is, in fact, often called 'reeling' – and to the tinkling of the alarm bell on a run-down electric clock.

Grasshopper warblers are small, olive-brown birds with much broken streaking on their backs. The best time to see them is during April and May, when the males (who are, as is usual with birds, the singers) are reeling from the top of a bush or a post to attract a female. After they have found a mate, they are more likely to sing from deep in the undergrowth. Moreover, they sing mainly when it is getting dark, sometimes going on until late into the night, or even into the dawn.

A difficulty for older people is that the grasshopper warbler's song is so high-pitched that they may not be able to hear it. For listeners who can, it seems to swell and sink in volume, or to come now from one place, now another. These effects are caused by the bird turning its head as it sings.

It is an elusive bird, spending much of its time hidden in bushes and reeds, but is not actually very shy. There is a record of a birdwatcher concealing himself near a regular song post. He stayed there until the bird began singing, then crept forward and actually touched the singer.

It used to be thought of as a bird of the marshes and other watery places. Those are still the best places to look for it, but in recent years it has been found more often in dry locations with plenty of low vegetation. It nests near or on the ground, under bushes such as brambles, and it likes undergrowth with close, accessible ground beneath, where it can look for food without coming out.

I have found that there is one other good way of finding a grasshopper warbler. When the bird is travelling repeatedly to and from its nest, either to build it or to feed the young, it usually approaches by a regular route, which may include a post or perching place. It does not like to fly down to its nest when it knows it is being observed, so it will stay on the post for a considerable length of time, making a sharp 'chick' note that is a little different from the comparable notes of birds such as robins. Hearing this note coming over the rushes or sedges may lead one to an easily observed grasshopper warbler.

I had an enjoyable shock beside the lake at Great Amwell in Hertfordshire. For several years a small colony of cormorants has nested in a weeping willow tree there. They are part of a general movement inland by cormorants, which were once birds only of the rocky sea cliffs. These birds have come up the river Lea in winter to fish and have stayed.

I saw the willow tree about six weeks ago. There were already a few cormorants standing in it, and one sitting on a bulky nest. But the whole tree, like the nests it held, was white. It had been completely coated with the guano produced by several generations of young birds. With its drooping shoots, it looked like an enormous white head of hair and seemed completely dead. The cormorants have killed it, I thought.

Cormorant

This week I was absolutely astonished. The whole tree was emerald green. The shoots were alive and all the leaves had come out. Only the nests were still white, lodged among the foliage. Now there were three birds on nests, with others standing in the twigs close by – sinister black figures amid the green – so the willow is not going to crumble away and the willow colony has a future.

The cormorants regularly fish in the lake, floating under the surface with only their heads and their gleaming green eyes visible before they sink down to chase their prey. However, it was midday when I arrived – a time when most birds have already had a good morning's feed and are taking a break. So the birds that were not sitting on a nest were just standing doing nothing, some on a sandbank with their wings spread out to dry.

The cormorants are evidently laying and beginning to incubate now. In the meantime they have other spring scenes around them to watch. That morning, newly arrived sedge warblers were popping up above the reeds; a pair of great crested grebes were facing each other on the water and displaying; and four tufted duck drakes were swimming in a square, with a female imprisoned in the middle. They were all waiting to see which of them she would choose as her mate, and they were sticking close to her side.

I had been wandering through some meadows by the river Stort, south of Bishop's Stortford, and looking at the cuckoo flowers, the first I had seen this year. These delicate pink flowers rising above the grass are supposed to bloom as the cuckoo arrives, so I was hoping they might bring me luck. And they did. Only a few minutes later, I heard the enthusiastic cry of a cuckoo ring out from behind a wood on the other side of the river. But I could not cross the river here and never saw the caller.

So far this year I have had to move around rather a lot to find some of the summer migrants, and in four cases I have only found a single one of them. One was this cuckoo.

A week earlier I saw my first swallow in a village in Northamptonshire. It was singing on the roof of a converted barn in the main street – perhaps it or its ancestors had once nested there.

I watched its bothered-looking, red face as it poured out a stream of twitters, always ending with a rattling trill and then a kind of snarl – a very curious song when you listen to it carefully. However, I have not seen another swallow yet, not even around the farms along the Stort.

I saw my first and only sedge warbler, also just over a week ago, in the Lea Valley – a spirited little bird, flinging itself into the air above a reed bed and singing its jerky song before dropping down again. It had a better chance of attracting a mate this way than if it had just stayed singing in the reeds, though it was doing that too.

The fourth singleton of the year was a lesser whitethroat. I heard this bird just after I had heard the cuckoo. You cannot mistake the lesser whitethroat's loud, explosive rattle. This particular bird was in some hawthorn bushes, but again on the far side of the river. The bird never emerged from the dense foliage, so I had to be content with hearing that one too.

No doubt I shall be seeing and hearing plenty more of these birds in the next few weeks. I think the early spring has inclined us to think that the summer migrants would be arriving early, but they seem in the main to be following their usual calendar. At any rate, in the woods alongside the river there were already many blackcaps and chiffchaffs singing. So as I walked along the towpath, I did have a frieze of summer song accompanying me all the way.

When you are watching golf from a seaside course on television, you can often hear a shrill piping of birds in the background. It is the sound of oystercatchers displaying on the beach, as they are doing now all around Britain.

These large black-and-white wading birds have a remarkable way of defending their territories on the shingle. If an intruding oystercatcher comes along, the owner of the territory hunches its shoulders, points its long red bill at the ground and starts piping. Then it runs at the intruder. Its mate usually joins it in the fight and other oystercatchers get carried away by the excitement and hurry along to take part too.

There may soon be six or seven birds in the party

(thirty have been recorded). They all run along, piping, side by side. Some fly about with their bills still pointing downwards. This is the source of the hullabaloo echoing over the golf course. It is not surprising that the intruder usually leaves.

Oystercatcher

The oystercatcher's feeding habits are also fascinating. Despite their name, they do not usually eat oysters but love other seafood. Their beaks are very strong and sharp, and can prise limpets off a rock – though they can also break a hole in a limpet shell with fierce blows. Above all, they are very skilful at opening mussels. They get their beaks between the two valves of the mussel and sever the ligament that holds them together.

But all this poking and hammering soon wears down the birds' beaks and you sometimes see them with a square end. The oystercatcher has evolved a remarkable solution for this. Their beaks renew themselves by growing very quickly – three times faster, it has been calculated, than human fingernails.

Most often, you just see them flying by with loud 'kleep' calls; sometimes inland, since in recent years they have taken to nesting on the grassy slopes of river valleys. The sitting birds look vulnerable there, but they generally manage to survive, even when clumsy sheep are wandering and nibbling all around them.

I have had one of my birding hopes fulfilled. The sun was warm and I was walking beside the river Stort, north of the ancient town of Sawbridgeworth in Hertfordshire, with newly arrived warblers singing everywhere in woods and copses around.

Chiffchaffs – slim, olive-brown birds that come late in March – were making their clinking 'chiff, chaff' song in the tallest trees. Lower down, blackcaps darted about, singing bursts of rich, passionate-sounding song; these silvery-grey birds with skullcaps had arrived in the past week. Coming from silver birches, I could hear the sweet, trickling songs of willow warblers, which are like chiffchaffs apart from their song. These had probably arrived from Africa that morning – they were not there the day before.

It was a wonderful accompaniment to the astonishingly summery weather. But for me, the best moment was still to come.

Suddenly, from a small hawthorn tree just in front of me on the river bank, there was a deafening outburst of song. I stepped forward quickly and there, on top of the tree, I saw a little rufous bird with a splash of white over its eye and a long, rounded tail. It was a Cetti's warbler. Originally Mediterranean birds, Cetti's warblers bred first in Britain in 1972 and have since spread through southern England, nesting beside rivers and lakes. They are famous for their song, now the loudest of all British bird songs, and the extraordinary difficulty one has in getting a good view of them.

In the Lea Valley I have often heard their lyrical shouts from deep in the reed beds, though never have I had more than a glimpse of one flitting over the water. I have also heard them beside Lake Como, singing in the brambles and olives. But they have always vanished before I reached the bush in which they were singing.

My bird on the hawthorn did not linger. It swept low over the river, giving me another good view of its long tail, then disappeared into the undergrowth. But at last I had seen a Cetti's warbler plain and clear!

Cetti's Warbler

Common terns, or sea swallows, are making their way north along the coast and up the rivers. They have spent the winter in West Africa and are now coming back to nest. They are delightful birds – silvery-white with a black cap – and, as they fly, they rise and fall with every stroke of their long, narrow wings. Behind them stream out the long, swallow-like feathers on each side of their tail.

They live on fish and catch them beautifully. They patrol the water, their red beaks pointing downward, then, when they spot a fish, spiral swiftly in the air and dive. They enter the water almost vertically and, if they are lucky, they come out with the fish flashing in their beak.

Fish play another part in their life. When a male gets back to his colony, he flies around in the sky in what ornithologists call his 'fish flight'. He carries a fish in his beak, making harsh cries, and a female may come up and fly beneath him. However, he does not give her the fish. It is only after a few days, when a pair has formed more firmly, that the male starts handing over. The pair flies down to the ground and there he presents her with the prize.

After that, things change, and when she starts egg-laying, he feeds her regularly. Then, when they are sitting on eggs in their ground nest, they take it in turns to feed each other.

Apart from their nests in colonies along the coast, common terns breed inland on gravel pits and other waters. They use sandy islands, or the large rafts that nowadays are specially made for them.

Another similar tern is also coming back to breed here at this time of year – and that is the Arctic tern. Some of these remarkable birds fly from the Antarctic to the Arctic Circle in spring and back again in autumn. In Britain they nest mostly in northern Scotland. They are best distinguished from the common tern by their pure red beaks, since the latter's has a black tip.

Birdwatchers have a witty name for the terns that they cannot confidently identify. They call them 'comic terns'.

May

In his poem 'Home Thoughts, from Abroad' Robert Browning dreams of the distant delights of the English countryside in April, then continues: 'And after April, when May follows, / And the whitethroat builds, and all the swallows!' I have always thought that 'when May follows' was rather slack padding, since May always follows April, but Browning was certainly right about the whitethroats.

These perky little warblers have been flocking back from Africa to the field-side hedges of Britain and are indeed about to begin building. They are brownish birds with a bulging silvery throat, a cocked tail and a loud, scratchy song. When the males first arrive they sing from deep in the hedges and emerge only after a few days when they have settled down. I heard my first one singing completely hidden behind a mass of snowy flowers on a long blackthorn hedge. As I walked along the hedge, it moved along inside ahead of me, singing continuously, and when I reached the end it turned back. It never put its head out once.

Whitethroat

By now, however, that bird will be jumping up out of the hedge and singing in the air. It will hang over the hedge, bouncing up and down like a puppet on an elastic string, then dropping jerkily down again. In this way it will proclaim its ownership of the hedge and invite a female to join it there.

As for building nests, the cock whitethroat is quite

unusual. It constructs up to five flimsy nests of grass and, once it has a mate, it invites her to choose one of them. The nests are often in nettle beds at the foot of a hedge and people rarely see them.

The cock's nests, as they are called, are decorated by the male with petals and spiders' cocoons to attract his mate. But she is more practical. Once she has chosen a nest, she strips off all the frippery, builds the nest up and settles down to raising her family there.

I have found my first nightingale. It was in a dense hawthorn thicket, just coming into flower, in the east of Hertfordshire. I had been watching a blackcap singing high in a tree when suddenly, fifty yards away, I heard the famous 'jug, jug, jug' ring out. 'Jug, jug, jug' is a supposedly poetic transcription of these notes, and one still often used. You have to pronounce 'jug' with the 'u' as in 'sugar' – but even then, of course, it is nothing like the real thing.

This _was_ the real thing. I forgot the blackcap and went in pursuit. A moment later there was a burst of rich, jangled notes from the thicket, so powerful and resonant that there could be absolutely no mistaking the singer. Between me and it, however, there ran a deep, muddy river, with no crossing anywhere near.

So I stood on the riverbank and waited. The bird was evidently moving about, since I very soon heard, now from some yards further off, the other major theme of the nightingale's song – the extraordinarily beautiful, sobbing 'piu, piu, piu'. It seemed to shake the whole thicket with its grief. Then there was silence.

But soon there was quite a different sound, coming from inside a forest of dry Himalayan balsam stalks that stretched between the river and the thicket – a harsh growling sound. This too, I knew, was the nightingale; this was its alarm call, as different from the song as it is possible to imagine.

It was evidently feeding on the ground now. In fact, I think it had probably arrived just that morning and was trying to eat and sing at the same time. Scraps of song came from it back in the hawthorns – now here, now there – and again I heard the 'jug, jug, jug', this time in all its passionate, throbbing intensity. I never saw the bird, unless some shadowy movements at the foot of the thicket can be counted. But that is a common enough experience with nightingales. A friend of mine actually heard six nightingales singing in Kent last week and did not see a single one.

What was really extraordinary was how my nightingale's song, even on the occasions when it just delivered a single note, completely eclipsed all the other songs around it. It was so overwhelming that a wren nearby was totally outclassed, while a robin seemed just to fade out of existence. As for my luckless blackcap, its beautiful song sounded no more than a sweet tinkling in the air on this remarkable nightingale morning.

I have been walking with a friend on Frensham Common, one of the great surviving stretches of gorse, heather and silver birches in Surrey. But we had a shock when we arrived: half the common was a black wasteland. There had been a terrible fire, we learnt, and where it had raged there were far-stretching acres of burnt soil with only a few black birch trunks scattered over it. Happily, the other half was unscathed, with paths of white sand separating it from the burnt area, and there was plenty of gorse in bright yellow flower.

We did not expect to see many birds, given what had happened, but we were lucky amid the gorse. Linnets were flying about making their sweet, twanging calls, and a stonechat with a glossy, black head came up and sat on top of a bush. A kestrel hovered for a moment overhead; sedge and reed warblers were singing in a reed bed beside Frensham Little Pond, and two common terns were diving into the water for fish.

We had hoped that we might see woodlarks, which are scarce relatives of the skylark and have an even lovelier song. As a boy I used to watch them circling over Smith's Lawn in Windsor Great Park, before it became a polo ground, and I once found a nest in the heather there. Their Latin name is *Lullula*, which echoes the beautiful, bell-like notes of their song. But above the common, the sky was silent.

Then, just in front of us, two birds flew up into a birch tree. As they faced us, we could see their streaky breasts and our first thought was that they were pipits – either meadow pipits or newly arrived tree pipits. But one turned sideways and their identity became plain. They had white stripes above their eyes that met on the back of their neck and stubby, little tails. They were a pair of woodlarks.

Moreover, one had some insects in its beak. So we had not heard a singing woodlark, but – even better – we had found a breeding pair. They must have had a nest with young in it just outside the burnt area. They were survivors of the fire and gave hope for the common and its future regeneration.

Many great tits are now sitting on eggs in their mossy nests inside tree holes and nestboxes. The news that they are adapting themselves individually to warmer springs is very good indeed, since it has been feared for a long time that climate change would lead to one of two possible disastrous results.

Great Tit

Great tits feed their young in the nest mainly on the caterpillars of the winter moth, which are found in vast numbers during springtime on the leaves of oak trees. Before the warmer springs began to occur, the hatching of the young great tits and the hatching of the caterpillars always more or less coincided, so there was food in abundance for the young birds.

The fears were that the early onset of warm weather would lead either to the caterpillars coming on to the leaves too early for the birds, or the birds coming into breeding condition too early for the caterpillars. Either of these situations would have caused havoc for the great tits.

The birds might, of course, have adjusted through the

process of evolution, with the better-adapted birds slowly becoming the majority of the great tit population. But that would have taken a very long time.

Now, however, Oxford scientists have shown that not only are the caterpillars appearing earlier, but the great tits have managed to adjust as individuals to the new situation by nesting sooner as well. Where the great tit is concerned, the community of nature has changed with its parts still in harmony with each other. So the future for these birds looks much more secure. And the discovery may prove to apply to other endangered birds too.

There have been two more interesting discoveries about birds. Julia Carter, a PhD student at Bristol University, has found that starlings know when people are looking at them. You can stand quite near a dish they are eating from and they will ignore you – until you turn your eyes on them. Then they move away. Perhaps they can always detect the attentive eyes of a predator.

In Madrid, research has revealed that blue tits can actually smell predators: when scientists there put the scent of a ferret into nest boxes that had chicks in them, the parent tits waited measurably longer before entering the dark boxes with food.

Altogether, it seems, birds can look after themselves better than we have previously realised.

Garden warblers are now singing vigorously in the woods. A few weeks ago their relatives the blackcaps were the predominant voices, but now the garden warblers, who arrived later, have taken over.

But some blackcaps are still singing, and it is not easy to distinguish between the two birds' songs. Even if you think that you have identified one successfully, it is often impossible to confirm it now that the foliage is thick on the trees – both species can lurk and sing among the leaves without giving even a glimpse of themselves.

After years of listening I think that I can generally pick out one from the other. The blackcap starts by muttering, then builds up to a wild, noisy, beautiful climax; the garden warbler's song is a more bubbling, evenly delivered song, which occasionally breaks into rich passages. Still, each species can sometimes give sustained performances of very melodious notes, and then it is very hard to be sure.

I have particularly vivid memories of both birds in song, though in each case the singer, rather unusually, was right out on a branch and clearly visible. On the Scottish island of Gigha, I once saw a garden warbler on top of a small tree singing as powerfully as a nightingale. In the forest of Fontainebleau, I watched a blackcap on a side-branch doing just the same.

Once they are seen there is no problem in telling the two apart. The male blackcap has – as its name suggests – a black skullcap (though the female's is brown). The garden warbler is distinguished by its having absolutely no distinguishing features; it is just a small, brown bird, paler below.

Last weekend I happened to be standing midway between a singing garden warbler and a singing whitethroat, two species that are also related. You could not confuse their songs, with the steady bubble of the first and the scratchy notes of the second; yet apart from these features there was a considerable likeness between the songs – a sort of characterless, warbling undertow. Probably all these warbler songs originate in something that was sung by a common ancestor and diverged with the evolution of the individual species.

Recently, several cases have been noted of willow warblers breaking into a kind of chiffchaff song, and chiffchaffs suddenly producing a willow-warbler-like song. In fact, if you speed up a recording of a chiffchaff, and slow down a willow warbler, each bird does sound rather like the other. A common ancestor again?

Woodcocks are very punctual birds. At present the males are flying round their woodland territories at sunset, just above the treetops, making soft groans and clicking calls. They go round and round on exactly the same route, and if you have discovered the route, you can wait confidently to see them.

Some years ago I drove down with some friends from London to Windsor Forest, where I knew one was performing; I assured them that I would show them a woodcock.

We arrived at the spot I had chosen and got out of the car. I looked at my watch and took a gamble. 'It will be here in three minutes,' I said. I was lucky. After exactly three minutes we looked up and there was the woodcock, flying overhead with its peculiar slow wing beats and clicking away with its long beak open. Triumph!

They go round to look for females in the wood below and when they hear a call from one in the undergrowth, they go down and court her. They may mate with three or four females in the course of the summer.

At other times, though, woodcocks are hard to see. They lie in the woods all day, beautifully camouflaged against the broken bracken and dead leaves. Sometimes people manage to spot their shining, black eyes, or a dog startles one and it flies up, crashing out through the undergrowth. Otherwise, they come out only at night, when they go down to meadows to feed quietly in the darkness, rocking to and fro as they probe deep into the ground with their beaks. However, some woodcocks were seen unexpectedly during the cold spell earlier this year when they appeared in gardens during the daytime, even in London, in search of food.

The females lay their four eggs on the ground, usually at the foot of a tree. It is said that they will carry their chicks out of danger, holding them between their thighs as they fly. For a long time this was thought to be a myth, but now there appear to be some reliable observations of these resourceful woodcocks. That is something to look for in the woods next month.

I have been bumping over the sea off south-west Wales in an open motor boat on my way to Grassholm, a rocky island ten miles out from St David's, and I was going there to see its great gannet colony.

In the south-easterly wind the sea was quite rough, but the sky was blue and the sun was warm. As the island came into view we could see that it was entirely white, as though a giant lace shawl had been thrown over it. Then it became clear that the lace consisted of thousands of nesting gannets on the island's slopes, all sitting so close together that they could have touched their neighbours with their beaks (but didn't). Each was sitting on a single egg, which would hatch early in June.

By now the sky, too, was full of these enormous birds – over four feet from wing tip to wing tip – swooping and gliding around us. They were a dazzling white in the sunshine and their yellowish heads looked like polished ivory. They had beaks like daggers, and tails as sharp-pointed as a needle.

But the sight on the rocks was even more spectacular. There are now 32,000 breeding pairs of gannets on Grassholm, a number that has grown year by year since the RSPB bought it sixty years ago. They have even encroached on the former landing place, so one cannot now go ashore.

A continuous roar comes from the island, as birds returning from the sea are greeted with growls by their mate on the nest. Couples rise up and touch beaks in greeting. Then the sitting bird goes off to feed, far out in the ocean. It will return twenty-four hours later and the pair will change places again. The birds constantly drop their guano all around them, so the rock gets whiter and whiter – and a terrible stench sometimes wafted across to our boat.

Many tiny guillemots stood among the gannets. They had not invaded the colony; rather it was the gannets that had encroached on the guillemots' traditional ledges. Grey seals sunbathed on the rocks. We sailed round to the windward side of the island. Here there were fewer nesters, but a vast cloud of non-breeding gannets rose into the sky. Some started diving for a shoal of mackerel. A swallow flitted daringly through the flock.

It was time for us to go, but anyone can make their own trip to Grassholm through a firm called Thousand Island Expeditions.

In many places the sky is full of starlings carrying food to the young in their nests. They fly straight and fast as they bring in beakfuls of insects that they have found in parks and fields. I have often thought that their name should mean 'little star', for in flight they are very much like four-pointed stars, but the etymologists will have none of this.

Starlings are always busy, noisy birds. When they are collecting food from the grass they run about rapidly as they look for it. They plunge their beaks into the ground, then push open the mandibles and fish around in the little slot that this makes.

I have had a letter from Mrs Sandra Hammerton saying she has watched starlings in her garden eating snails. Snails appear in bird books in lists of starling food, but starlings are not often seen tackling them. Song thrushes break the shells open on a stone, but Mrs Hammerton's starlings impale the snails on their beaks, then 'shake and rub the snail on the garden path until they are able to winkle it out of its shell'. A few more thumps on the ground and then they eat it.

By now, most starling pairs have got quite large young-sters in the nest, and these are just as energetic. As soon as they hear the scratch of their parents' feet outside the nest hole, the young birds burst into a loud, churring chorus, all begging to be fed. It is one of the most characteristic sounds of the second half of May.

By the beginning of June, most of the young starlings will be out of the nest. Starlings in a neighbourhood form a kind of loose colony that coordinates its breeding season, so all the young birds emerge together and go off with their parents to the fields in flocks. Here again the fledglings put everything they have got into being fed. They chase their parents about, squawking energetically, and when the parent they are pursuing flies up they set off after it, still squawking.

The young are easily distinguished from the adults because they are plain, brown birds with a white throat. After three weeks they are ready to fend for themselves, and then they entirely abandon their parents. They go off in juvenile flocks and one comes across them in lonely sheep fields and cow pastures, all running about round the animals' feet.

Meanwhile, for most of the adults the summer's work is done. They join up in their own flocks, and in the afternoon all of them sing together in bushes or high on pylons, having a little leisure at last.

I have just seen a symbolic sight in the Hertfordshire skies. A buzzard was soaring far away over a wood, and quite near it a raven was slowly circling too.

Raven

Buzzards are now quite a familiar sight, even in low-lying counties such as Hertfordshire, sailing overhead and mewing, their wings lifted, as they look for rabbits below.

But it was the raven flying alongside the buzzard that made the sight astonishing. Seeing the two together reminded me of the W. H. Davies poem in which he registers his wonder and joy at hearing a cuckoo calling while there is a rainbow in the sky: 'A rainbow and a cuckoo's song / May never come together again; / May never come / This side the tomb.'

Yet the buzzard and the raven may come together again – and more and more often. For what has happened to the buzzard now seems to have started happening to the raven.

Until lately, ravens were breeding birds of hills and cliffs in the West, rarely seen elsewhere. But now their nests are eating away at the map of the Midlands, and occasionally birds are seen as far east as Cambridgeshire and Norfolk.

Normally, ravens are not all that easy to distinguish from carrion crows at a distance, since their main difference is their greater size – and size is hard to judge when a bird is far away. But this black bird sailing high in the sky was quite close to the buzzard and you could see that it was distinctly bigger. That meant it had to be a raven.

And although such details as the raven's little beard, and even its powerful beak, were impossible to make out, its characteristic wedge of a tail was discernible.

So, a buzzard and a raven flying together in an eastern county – a symbol of a future that is probably on its way.

June

Everywhere now there is a thin chattering to be heard among the leafy branches of the trees. It is the sound of young blue tits calling out for food. Many have come out of the nest. But they are still dependent on their parents. They do not chase their parents as the young starlings do, but instead sit on a twig, calling and waiting.

Sometimes they sit out quite openly in the sunshine and it is easy to distinguish them. As well as being fluffy with shorter tails, they have yellow cheeks, whereas the adults' cheeks are white. In fact, the fledglings have an altogether yellower look, and their cap is more green than blue.

There are often six or seven young birds in the family and their parents have to work hard to feed them. This is why it is still important to put out peanuts and fat in the summer – it makes it easier and quicker for the adult blue tits to feed themselves while looking for caterpillars for their brood.

Oak trees are the main source of the all-important caterpillars. Many species of moth lay their eggs on oaks and soon after the fresh, green leaves appear the eggs hatch and the caterpillars start eating them. The earliest to appear are the caterpillars of the tiny, green tortrix moth, which hide themselves in rolled-up leaves, fastened by silk. This does not prevent the adult blue tits from finding them, however. Then there are the 'looper' caterpillars of the geometrid moths, so called because they arch their bodies as they make their way along – these look like twigs. A larger caterpillar that also camouflages itself is that of the great oak beauty moth, which looks even more twig-like than the looper as it sticks itself out, stiff and motionless, from the side of a real twig.

These disguises do not easily fool the tits, though – and at this time the caterpillars are really abundant. Many drop down from the branches on silken threads. If you walk through an oak wood you may feel the threads brushing your face and find a caterpillar on your shoulder or your ear – which may not please you as much as it would a blue tit.

I have been watching a family of kingfishers at the Rye Meads RSPB reserve in Hertfordshire. The young birds had fledged the day before and they and their parents were lurking around a pool where they had nested in a hole in an artificial sandbank.

Kingfisher

My first sighting from my hide was a flying bird. Or could it really be a bird? It was like a bolt of brilliant, blue light streaking away across the water into the trees. Next moment another one landed on a stick in the water just in front of me and gave me a spectacular close-up. That bolt of light had seemed very long, yet here was a tiny bird, no bigger than a chaffinch. But it was one of the most vividly coloured birds in the world, with a gleaming, electric-blue back, a broken white collar and rich orange underparts.

I was close enough to see the red at the base of its black beak that showed it to be a female.

I slowly became aware of other members of the family. A surprising thing about kingfishers is that the broken colour of their plumage camouflages them in foliage. I detected one on a shadowy willow branch, but when I took my eye off it I lost it. Then I noticed an orange reflection in the water beneath some bushes – and in the bushes, sure enough, I made out another one. Yet another flew out of the trees and a magpie shot out behind and chased it. The kingfisher was probably a young one – the cunning magpie must have seen that it was inexperienced. But it got away.

In other years I have watched these birds fishing in a large lake nearby. I remember one that sat very still in an overhanging hawthorn. Kingfishers have amazing adjustable eyes that can see all around them or, alternatively, focus on every movement in the water. Suddenly it plunged in and came up, water pouring off it, with a shining fish in its beak. It landed, beat the fish on a branch and swallowed it.

Young kingfishers can fish from their first day out, and I am sure that my family are now all over the Rye Meads lakes doing just that.

In tall birch and beech woods – now in brilliant, full green leaf – a strange song can sometimes be heard coming down from the treetops. It is a shivering call, like the equivalent in sound of shimmering light. It also has a second phase that the singer occasionally breaks into – a sad-sounding 'piu, piu, piu...' like an ethereal version of the nightingale's rich, melancholy outburst.

The singer is a wood warbler, the largest of our so-called 'leaf warblers', the other two being the willow warbler and the chiffchaff. Of the three, it is the one most aptly called a leaf warbler, since it is the brightest green, especially in early June when its colour above closely matches that of the leaves among which it sings. Its throat is yellow and its underparts pure white; looking up, you can sometimes glimpse these colours through the foliage.

The wood warbler's nesting habits are rather strange and, one might think, rather risky. As a rule, tall beeches and birches do not have many lower branches, or much undergrowth beneath them. The beech woods, especially, can be like dark caverns. Yet wood warblers nest on the ground, making a domed nest of grass in a hollow in the leaf mould, with little or no cover, so they have to drop the last few yards to the ground to their nests without the sheltered approach that most birds have.

I have watched them when they are coming down with nesting material, and also later when they are bringing food to their young. They descend to the lowest bough near the nest and wait there cautiously until the coast is clear. Then, very swiftly, they drop. It looks very rash, but whenever I have watched them from a distance through field glasses they have always got away with it.

Another attractive feature of these little birds is the male's display flight in front of the female in early summer. He flies past her with his green wings beating faster than usual, but somehow managing at the same time to move more slowly. If I were asked to choose the bird that was most like the spirit of the woods in June, I would certainly choose the wood warbler.

The song of the nightjar is one of the most haunting sounds of June evenings. In the twilight, from woodland clearings or on heaths with birches and small conifers, you hear this soft, rather wooden whirring; now near, now far away, and going on and on. The apparent coming and going of the sound is caused by the nightjar turning its head as it sings. Its song post is either a prominent tree branch or on the top of a small tree.

One is most likely to see the nightjar when it flies about at dusk catching moths and beetles. It glides and wheels on its long wings, a dark shape but, in the case of the male, showing three white wing-spots and some white at the edge of its tail. These marks are conspicuous even in the gloom. As it flies it often makes loud 'coo-ic' calls. It also displays in the dusk, clapping its wings above its back to court its mate and to warn rivals to keep away.

Nightjar

In the daytime the nightjar can be very hard to see. It lies low, sometimes on a branch, where to make itself less conspicuous, it will stretch along it, not across it. More often it just lies on the ground among the dead, brown bracken and the new, green bracken shoots. Its intricate streaking and mottling – black and brown and cream – are perfect camouflage for it here. It even keeps its eyes half-closed to make it less visible.

However, once or twice I have seen one on the ground and been able to marvel at this camouflaging. On each occasion, I was walking carefully among some small Douglas firs and new bracken, where I knew there were nightjars, and my movement flushed one out. It landed again, not far away, and I marked the spot. As I approached, I managed to detect the nightjar lying perfectly still with its body somehow shrunken, which helped to conceal it even better.

It lays its two eggs in just such places, with the female doing most of the incubating, although the male relieves her for a while at dusk and dawn.

With trees growing tall or being felled, the nightjar arrives and disappears again in different places over the years, but where the habitat is stable it returns from Africa to the same stretch of ground each summer.

I knew a pub landlord in Suffolk who used to stand by his door with a glass at closing time every summer, telling his customers 'I'm hearing a nightjar, and having a night jar' while listening to its call.

The swifts are back again over my garden in north London. I never tire of watching them in the evening as they sweep across the sky, first gliding, then propelling themselves with a fevered burst of wing beats. They are like fine black arcs; but on clear evenings the setting sun catches the underside of their wings with a bronze glow.

Sometimes there are two of them, occasionally a third,

and from time to time another swirl of half a dozen comes in from further away. I think the two birds are a pair, one of them leaving the eggs for a short while to join its mate. The third may also have a mate on its eggs. But I do not know under which roof in this densely built-up neighbourhood they have their nests.

This weekend their eggs are probably hatching. The swifts lay at the middle or end of May and the eggs take about three weeks to hatch.

Few people have seen the inside of a swift's nest. One place where their nests have been watched is in the tower of the University Museum of Natural History, Oxford. This astonishing neo-Gothic tower has a high, pyramidal roof with numerous ventilator shafts, which the swifts have taken over as nesting sites. Nowadays there are about sixty pairs breeding there; what the birds do not know is that for sixty years they have been nesting in specially made boxes into which observers can look.

The late Dr David Lack began watching the swifts in 1948 and published his remarkable book about them, *Swifts in a Tower*, in 1956. He saw how a swift on the nest would deal with an intruder, rising on its feet and screaming, then advancing towards the stranger with its wings half-opened. The intruder usually fled. He saw how the pairs preened each other – courtship that also helped to keep their feathers in good shape for flying. And he watched them feed their young – endlessly bringing in a new ball, or bolus, of flying insects in their throats.

Visitors to the museum can now see what Lack saw, for it has a monitor screen with cameras trained on four of the nests. And it is well worth visiting the museum itself, which also has the most complete remains of a single dodo anywhere in the world.

Just after they arrived back in England in mid-May, I had some superb views of a pair of hobbies feeding in the sky over a lakeside wood. I was watching from a hide on the opposite side of the lake and for an hour I saw them gliding and swooping in pursuit of insects, no doubt including dragonflies that had been swept up from the water. Hobbies are small falcons with curved-back wings, and when they sped towards me on the wind they looked more like a bow than an arrow. As they suddenly dropped like stones – just as a peregrine falcon does – to pick up something alongside the wood, I could see their blue and black colour clearly against the green foliage.

By now, the female is probably sitting on her eggs in an old crow's nest, quite at home here. But what will they be doing when they are back in Africa for our winter? Until recently, no one knew; however, in 2008, and again in 2009, some German ornithologists tracked a female hobby from an old raven's nest in a pine tree near

Berlin to the woods and savannah in Angola, where it lived from October to March. They fastened a tiny satellite transmitter to the hobby's back. This weighed only 5g (with a harness of 1g), compared to the bird's 265g, and never seemed to give it any trouble. It recorded an extraordinary journey.

The distance the hobby flew to the southernmost point it reached was 10,065km (6,250 miles). The bird spent forty-nine and forty-two days respectively in the two years on its autumn migration, travelling for an average of about 250km a day. Once in southern Africa it roamed for enormous distances through the woods, a total of almost 10,000km each time, including excursions into Namibia and Zimbabwe.

On migration it probably caught swallows and swifts that were also migrating; in winter, it will have eaten termites. And each spring, travelling faster, it came back to its German home. It may be sitting on its eggs in the raven's nest again as you read this. So there we have a unique and amazing snapshot of what is, from our point of view, a hobby's winter holiday.

I was walking through a buttercup meadow beside a river when a bird sped over my head. Without really seeing it,

I took it to be a swallow. A moment later it made a sharp clicking note, as though it had read my mind and was saying as it shot away: 'No, I'm not, I'm a house martin.' The click was unmistakable.

Swallows often feed low over fields, but house martins tend to feed higher in the sky except when they fly around the legs of sheep and cows that are pulling up insects from the grass. Perhaps I had been doing that. Anyway, it disappeared – probably back to the town nearby, where I knew house martins were nesting under the eaves of several buildings.

Those brilliantly constructed mud nests are very much the centre of house martins' lives in summer and as long as there are flying insects around, they like to feed in the sky nearby. They have one of the smallest territories of all birds – about 6in (15cm) around the nest – but here they will fight off other house martins fiercely, whether the intruders are trying to take over the nest or merely steal a feather from the lining.

What, in particular, makes their nest a home is the fact that they use it to bring up their second brood. Not many blackbirds or other small birds use their nest twice. After one brood has been reared in it the average nest in a hedge is too battered and full of faeces and fleas to use again; if the owners want a second brood they build a new nest. But that would mean long labour for a pair of house martins, which, if they were lucky, would have already found an old nest that was practically intact when they arrived in the spring. In fact, a pair often uses its own nest from the previous year. So now they make do with the conditions inside it for their second family.

What also makes that nest a home is that the young birds of the first brood continue to roost in it with their parents. They gather in friendly flocks on overhead wires in the daytime, but go home at night. The nest can be a crowded place by the time September comes and the families start thinking of going back to Africa.

There is one bird of which almost half the British population is now breeding in nest boxes. No, it is not the blue tit or the great tit; it is the pied flycatcher.

To see this lively little summer visitor you must live in, or go to, the north or west of Britain, where it lives mainly in the oak woods along a line up from Devon to Dumfries. It is a typical flycatcher, darting out from a perch to catch flying insects, but the male is quite different from the more widespread spotted flycatcher. He is completely black and white – black above, shining white beneath, with a white wing bar – while the female is brown in the places where her mate is black.

They used to nest in holes in trees, but in the 1970s many people started putting nest boxes up on the tree trunks for them. The flycatchers did not hesitate to move in massively, especially in Wales and the Lake District. Since then, the number of pied flycatchers nesting in Wales has doubled – it now provides a home for two fifths of the British population of 55,000 – while the Cumbrian population has spilt over into south-west Scotland.

Pied Flycatcher

One problem is that the tits start nesting before the flycatchers arrive, so they get to the boxes first. To combat this, in some forests the wardens fill the boxes with rags until the singing male flycatchers arrive in the second half of April. They have a simple song with a few sweet notes, and stop singing when they get a mate – or two.

A curious characteristic of these birds is that soon after they have finished nesting the male turns brown, like the female. One September I was in a garden in the south of France, where many pied flycatchers were passing through. They flicked their wings upwards and made 'tick, tick' calls as usual, but every one of them was brown. It gave me a very odd feeling, as if something sinister had happened to the world.

A brief foray into the Lammermuir Hills south of Edinburgh last weekend produced an agreeable little clutch of moorland birds.

It was a grey but soft afternoon; warm, with the air sweet and almost still. As soon as we set foot on a sheep path through the heather, a meadow pipit climbed up jerkily into the sky, making a zipping note, and sailed down again with its wings lifted, now singing a snatch of more plummy song. A moment later a skylark was singing overhead.

Then, far away, we heard a wild trilling, that amazing chorus of bubbling notes, more and more passionately repeated, of a curlew flying round its territory. A carrion crow soared over and a lapwing flew up sharply, then swooped down on the crow several times. No doubt the lapwing had some chicks in a nest below, but the crow did not seem to think it worth hunting for them in the face of this attack and it sped away. The lapwing eyed us, then flopped off too.

A flicker of wings revealed a wheatear, an unmistakable bird when you see it from behind, with a conspicuous black T-shape on a white background at the end of its tail. It landed on the wall of a 'fank' – a circular sheep enclosure, beautifully made of stones. There was a stonechat bobbing on the fank's wall, too.

Now a clicking call came from a boggy bit of hillside where the white tufts of cotton grass were growing. It was the call a snipe usually makes when it is displaying over its territory, though it sometimes calls from the ground.

But the bird we particularly wanted to see was a red grouse. We were afraid that the grouse might be higher up in the hills, staying low in the heather with their young around them. Then, suddenly, we got our wish. Just a yard or two ahead of us, a brilliant head popped up above the heather – a gleaming eye, rufous feathers and a wonderful scarlet wattle above the eye. Bird books do not give much mention to this last feature, probably because one usually sees grouse as they fly away. However, it was the most colourful thing we saw that day and we felt very satisfied as we wove our way cautiously down the Lammermuirs again through a rising mist.

July

An extraordinary sight can be seen sometimes on mudflats in July. It is the march of the shelduck families from their rabbit burrows to the sea.

Shelducks – large birds midway between a duck and a goose – look black and white from a distance. At closer quarters you can see that their heads are actually a shiny green and that they have a chestnut breast-band, a scarlet beak and pink legs, when these are not covered in mud.

They nest mainly in rabbit burrows in sand dunes, but also in such places as crevices under beach huts. The female lays an enormous clutch of eggs – as many as fifteen – on a bed of down plucked from her breast. Sometimes another shelduck who has no nest will add her eggs, too. So a family of as many as twenty ducklings can emerge from the nest.

They are striking little things, with marbled brown-

and-white bodies and a brown cap. They can walk almost as soon as they are out of the egg and they all set off in a long line with their parents to the water. At low tide, this may be miles away, but they plod gallantly on, the mother generally leading and the father hovering about. It is a wonderful sight to go and look for on estuaries and muddy shores in July.

Shelduck

Later in the summer, there is another spectacular shelduck sight to be seen. Many of the adults fly off to the German coast to moult. They gather especially in the Heligoland Bight, where, without their flight feathers, they feel safe out on the vast stretches of mud. However, they leave their offspring behind. So back here crowds of young shelducks assemble along the shore in crèches, with only a few adults (called aunties) keeping an eye on them.

New marinas and harbours have wrecked some of the muddy shores where shelducks feed between the tides, but their numbers have so far managed to survive this assault and recently they have started breeding near inland waters. So you may even come across a line of infant shelducks tramping through the heart of the British countryside.

I was walking through some wheat fields near Baldock in Hertfordshire. On the rolling hills around me the wheat stalks were tightly packed and blue and the ears were ripening. In spite of the recent drought, it looked as if there would be quite a good harvest here.

It was very quiet, except for a skylark singing somewhere far above. Then I heard a soft 'see-ip' note just to the right of me. I swung my field glasses round and, almost at once, lit on a yellow wagtail swaying on top of the ears. It was obviously a male, with its bright yellow face and breast and its olive upper parts. Then I heard the same call coming from a little further off. Just as quickly, I found a paler-yellow female.

It was pretty evident that the pair had young nearby, either still in a nest on the ground or lurking among the stalks, and that they were warning them about me. The male flitted ahead, and every time I stepped a little further, he flew a bit further too. I felt he was trying to lead me away from their hidden chicks. And, indeed, I never saw them – if there was a nest it was probably at the edge of one of the tramlines left by farm vehicles through the crop.

It was delightful to come across these wagtails, now becoming scarce, but a few years ago I had an even better experience in a field nearby. I heard a yellow wagtail call and saw it land, again on top of some wheat. But this bird had a bright blue cap and a white eye-stripe. It was a blue-headed wagtail – a closely related, Continental subspecies that occasionally visits southern England. It flew off, but returned a moment later with a beakful of insects. Then I noticed a brownish wagtail sitting close by on another ear of wheat – a young bird. So my blue-headed wagtail had bred here; a very uncommon event. It had probably mated with a female yellow wagtail.

In spring, and again in autumn, yellow wagtails like feeding around the feet of farm animals in the fields, and when I see them, I always think of their wonderful French name, *bergeronnette printanière*, or spring shepherdess.

A few red-necked phalaropes have been appearing in unexpected places. They are amazing little wading birds that nest in summer beside lakes in the far north of Europe and prefer swimming about like coots to walking like other waders. What is most extraordinary is that the female is far more glamorous than the male, and lives a distinctly independent life. This is very rare in birds.

Red-Necked Phalarope

She is brown and grey, with a broad, brilliant orange patch down the side of her neck and a white throat. The male is a much duller version of her. Also, after laying her eggs in their waterside nest, she leaves incubation and the care of the young entirely to her mate. This peculiar situation has probably evolved because the northern summer is so short. Egg-laying uses up a lot of energy in a female and it is better that the male should take over the hard work for the rest of the season if they are to bring up their chicks successfully. In fact, red-necked phalaropes start leaving their breeding grounds at the end of June.

One or two pairs usually nest in Britain, in the Hebrides and Shetland Isles, but I have watched them mainly in Iceland. From my hotel beside the great Lake Mývatn I could walk down to the shore, dodging a fierce bombardment by Arctic terns nesting nearby, and see the phalaropes swimming about, heads held high, at the water's edge. They often performed their most famous trick, which is to spin round in the water, stirring up small creatures at the bottom that they can then eat.

Mývatn, incidentally, is a wonderful lake for other birds, with whooper swans trumpeting out on the water, gorgeous Slavonian grebes with black and orange heads nesting in the reeds, and snow buntings singing briskly from roofs.

As for the phalaropes, the other remarkable thing about them is the difference between their summer and winter lives. When they leave their breeding grounds, they fly to the Middle East and spend their winter in the warm water of the oceans south of Arabia.

Golden orioles are brilliant golden birds with black wings, unmistakable if you see them. But can you see them? Across the Continent there are millions of them, but here we are at the extreme north-western edge of their range. A few appear in spring, and several pairs usually nest in the Fen country – but that is all.

Even when they are around, they are very elusive. I have only found one for myself in Britain, and my experience was typical. I was staying one May in a village in Oxfordshire and as the sun went down, I suddenly heard in the distance the loud, fluting song of the male. It is a very attractive call, which I can only transcribe inelegantly as a 'woodley-woop'. I set off in search of the bird, but the call moved around in the dusk and I never got anywhere near to the caller. I got up early the next day and was delighted to hear the call ringing out again. Then the same thing happened as on the previous evening – as soon as I got anywhere near, the call stopped, and next minute I heard it coming from somewhere else. Not only do orioles lurk deep in the branches, but they fly very swiftly away from any potential approaching danger.

However, I was lucky. After a good hour trailing after the bird, I found myself getting quite close to it in a small wood. And there, suddenly, I saw it – perched, untypically but very helpfully, on the top of a cypress tree. It was not golden and black but green and black, but it was an undoubted oriole. In fact, the females and younger birds are a yellowish green, so mine, I concluded, was a juvenile male that was already in song.

Golden Oriole

The place to look for golden orioles is in and around the RSPB's Lakenheath Fen reserve in Suffolk. For the past thirty years they have been nesting in this area among plantations of hybrid black poplars. There were forty-two pairs in 1990. Since then their numbers have declined, mainly because mature poplars have been cut down for timber and not replaced – poplar wood is used for boxes and veneers, but the demand is not high.

Nevertheless, several pairs are generally found breeding there each summer. Even those are hard to see, with their elusive ways and their nests hidden high in the leafy treetops. But Lakenheath is there, waiting to be searched by anybody – and even if those maddening orioles never show, there is every chance of seeing marsh harriers, bearded tits and even common cranes as compensation.

I have been on a hunt for quails. The quail eggs you can buy in supermarkets come from farmed Japanese quails, but the birds I was looking for were wild European quails.

Quails are like tiny partridges that lurk in arable fields and hardly ever come out to show themselves. Every spring a few of them come to Britain from the Mediterranean, and every summer some more arrive. One theory about these later arrivals is that they have already nested further south and have come here to nest again. Another is that they are the offspring of birds that have nested further south and are themselves breeding now. Quails – unusually for birds – are known to be mature at three months old.

Anyway, one or two had been heard calling in a pea field beneath a chalky eminence called Deadman's Hill, near Baldock in Hertfordshire. I walked through miles of rolling fields full of ripening barley and wheat to get there, thinking, rather hopelessly, that the quails might have moved into any of them. But eventually I found Deadman's Hill and there, sure enough, was a field of peas, the pods fat and the leaves turning yellow.

Although few people ever see a wild quail, one can often hear them. They have a soft call that goes something like 'tip-i-tip', which is traditionally transcribed – probably by sweating farmworkers – as 'wet-mi-lips'.

I walked along a path beside the pea field, with skylarks singing in the clear sky overhead, and suddenly heard the delicate sound I so wanted to hear: 'Tip-i-tip, tip-i-tip.' It was coming from among the peas about twenty yards away. I scrutinised the spot intensely with my field glasses, but it was impossible to see anything among the dense, sprawling pea plants. I ventured out carefully, but the call moved away.

When I saw a little brown bird fly up, it was only another skylark. After that I heard no more, though I waited a very long time with the hot sun blazing down on me.

But I had managed to find my quail – my piping needle in a haystack. Next summer, I thought, by hook or by crook, I'll flush you, little bird. But now I too needed to wet my lips.

Green sandpipers are starting to appear in ones and twos at the edge of freshwater pools. They are coming down from northern Europe, and these first birds are probably from Finland. They are also most likely females, who often leave their chicks in the care of the males.

They are medium-sized waders with quite long legs, and their hindquarters bob up and down as they probe the mud in shallow water. Their backs are dark brown, with a faint, green gloss that you can hardly ever see, but they look almost black by contrast with their shining white underparts.

One often spots these birds first when they fly up. They have a white rump that, with the dark back, makes them look like large house martins, and they go up almost vertically, making a distinctive triple cry with a melancholy air to it. But it is worth waiting after they have disappeared over the horizon. If they have found a good feeding place, they will circle round and suddenly dive out of the sky again to resume wading just where they left off.

Unlike most waders – which on migration stop to feed along the coast or on estuaries – green sandpipers travel across land and like feeding in fresh water. They will come down at any inviting pool they see below. I have found them several times at small ponds in parks, and once I flushed a pair from the edge of a small river that ran between two fields in farmland. They were on a muddy patch where cows had come down to the water to drink and had trampled down the bank. They quickly came back again.

Even on estuaries you do not find them out on the mud and sand, but in the shallow dykes behind the seawall. They can drop in almost anywhere in Britain during July and August, and on bird reserves where there is a 'scrape' – a shallow stretch of mud and water deliberately created to attract ducks and waders, generally with a hide beside it – there is a very good chance of seeing them. They can stay here for a month or two, taking it easy in the summer weather, before moving on south.

A pair of green sandpipers has occasionally nested in Scotland, but they breed mostly in the boggy forests of the far north of Europe and Asia. Most unusually for a wader, they nest in trees. They do not make their own nests, however; instead they use old thrush or woodpigeon nests, and sometimes will even lay their eggs on a comfortable clump of witches' broom.

Sometimes one goes out expecting to see certain birds and comes home having seen something entirely different and unexpected. It happened like that last weekend. I was visiting Sawbridgeworth marsh, a nature reserve on the Essex–Hertfordshire border. As I had hoped, there was a fine display of purple marsh orchids just inside the gate, beside a soggy path, and among them some yellow rattle flowers, many with the round seed pods that rattle when you shake them.

I rattled one. But otherwise the marsh was strangely silent. I had thought there would be some sedge warblers singing in the reeds, managing a few beautiful notes with the right hand, as it were, then falling back, as always, on their clanking, grunting bass line. But not a sound was to be heard. However, one sedge warbler did suddenly appear at the top of the reeds, giving me a good view of its distinctive yellow eyebrow – and the insects in its beak showed why that one, at any rate, was preoccupied.

There was not even a reed bunting singing, though the cock birds often sit on a bulrush endlessly repeating their dry song – something like 'chizz, chizz, chizzy-wiz'. The marsh was proving unproductive. So I went on into the other part of the reserve, a rather open wood of old crack willow trees.

Suddenly, I was surrounded by birds that have nothing to do with the marshes I had come to see. There was a flash of silver and a treecreeper landed at the base of the gnarled trunk of one of the willows. What I had seen were its silvery underparts. But I did not see much more of it, since it quickly circled round to the far side of the trunk, and by the time I had got round myself, it had gone.

Then I heard in the willows a soft version of the long-tailed tit's lip-smacking note. It was a parent warning its brood that I had come on the scene. A moment later a whole troupe of young ones flitted across the path, their tails bouncing up and down.

A dark-brown shape rose from the ground, swept out of the wood and landed in a sallow bush beside the marsh. All I could see of it as it crouched there was a brown back and a long, barred tail. But there was no mistaking that tail – it belonged to a sparrowhawk. Perhaps the bird had caught one of the tits and was settling down half-hidden to rest and digest.

Finally, I did hear a reed bunting and picked it out, sitting perkily on a reed, its black head-feathers tousled. In the end, I felt, I had had the best of two habitats – or of two worlds.

Visitors to the seaside might like to look out for two uncommon species of gull, which, if they are lucky, they could see without moving from the beach. These are the yellow-legged and the Mediterranean gulls.

Yellow-legged gulls are very like the herring gulls that are so common along the coast. In the past, in fact, they were considered to be merely a subspecies of the herring gull, and they have only just been recognised as a separate species. You will find them mentioned only in the latest bird guides.

They stand out because of their rich yellow legs; herring gulls' legs are normally pink. The yellow-legged gull also has a darker grey back than the herring gull – though it is not as dark as the lesser black-backed gull – and it has more black on the wing tips.

The yellow-legged gull used to be mainly a

Mediterranean species. On the airport boat that takes you across the water to Venice, you can see them standing all along the way on the wooden poles that mark out the route. Recently, they have started nesting on cliff ledges and roofs in seaside towns further north, and from late July to September there is usually quite an influx of wandering yellow-legged gulls into Britain. There have even been a couple of attempts at breeding here – one bird hybridised with a lesser black-backed gull, to which it may be more closely related than to the herring gull, in spite of appearances. Indeed, if you see what looks like a herring gull consorting with some lesser black-backs over the sea, it is worth giving it a good scrutiny, since it may well prove to be a yellow-legged instead.

The Mediterranean gull is like that other common British gull, the black-headed gull. It too has a black head in summer. However, the black-headed gull's hood is more like a face mask, not extending to the back of the neck, whereas the Mediterranean gull's hood completely covers the whole head. Mediterranean gulls are also slightly bigger and look very white, without the black-headed's black wing tips. They have a red beak and red legs like the black-headed gull, but their beak is thicker and their legs are longer.

Mediterranean gulls have gone further than yellow-legged gulls and now breed here, with about 100 pairs nesting each year, mainly on the south coast but also in Scotland and Ireland. They often nest in black-headed gull colonies. Like the yellow-legged gulls, they have added a new interest to gull-watching in this country.

As July comes to an end there is generally the last chance of hearing skylarks singing. They are still around in the fields and have only just brought up the last of their young, but they are beginning to moult, and most of them are not trying to defend their territories any more.

When skylarks are singing high in the sky, they are actually keeping an eye on a well-defined patch of field or moorland directly below them and telling other skylarks to keep out. If they see another skylark – one other than their mate – go walking briskly into their patch or crossing the sky above it, they swiftly drop down to chase it out. Sometimes they will come down onto a fence to sing and warn another skylark off.

It was believed for a long time that birds kept a territory in summer mainly to provide food for their young. Now it is thought that keeping rival males away from their mate is often more important to them. Blackbirds, for instance, defend a nesting territory, but often feed and collect food outside it. However, during the breeding season the skylark appears to gather seeds and insects mainly in its own nest patch.

It has the kind of 'food territory' that earlier naturalists believed in.

By now, though, skylarks are foraging more widely, eating such items as buttercup seeds. When the harvest begins the skylarks will hope to pick up scattered grain, which has for centuries been at the top of their diet. However, they get less of it these days – scythes and the old reaper-binders left a lot of grain on the ground, and even in winter there was often a certain amount lingering on the stubble fields. Combine harvesters leave far less behind, and where they do leave some, the earth is soon ploughed up and the winter wheat is sown. Nowadays the skylarks eat the leaves of the winter wheat instead.

Our resident skylarks tend to stay alone around the fields where they nested, and there is usually a brief reprise of song from September to November. The singers seem to be reminding their neighbours that they will be back again in the New Year.

Meanwhile, many skylarks from the Continent pass over Britain in the autumn and there are always some winter visitors here. These fly around in flocks that swirl this way and that over the fields as though they were blown about by the wind. Our skylarks keep aloof from them. They will take up their territories and start singing seriously again as the days lengthen after Christmas.

August

I have been on Fair Isle, the three-mile-long rocky island between Orkney and Shetland, and I have been watching some powerful birds. The outstanding birds of the island are the skuas – two kinds: the great skua or 'bonxie' and the Arctic skua. They glide endlessly over the moors and cliffs, as confident on the wing when the wind howls and buffets as they are when the sea is breaking idly on the rocks.

The bonxies are magnificent, heavy shouldered birds, dark brown with a white streak on the wing. They reminded me of enormous white admiral butterflies. They like to carry off the puffins that nest in burrows on the cliff tops, for a meal of one puffin a day is enough for them. They also steal fish from other seabirds, and occasionally a rogue bird will attack lambs.

The Arctic skuas are instantly distinguishable from them. They are much more lightly built, with narrow, gull-like wings, and they twist and turn brilliantly in the air when chasing a gull that has a fish in its beak. Most of them have plumage very similar to the bonxie's, but there is another form that has a white breast and a dark cap.

Both species still have young among the heather and they are fierce when you approach these. They fly menacingly around and if you get too close they will swoop down, sometimes touching your head. Once a bonxie attacked me in an even more dramatic way, coming at me low over the heather until we were looking into each other's eyes, and only swerving up at the last minute – alarming, but I survived.

The puffins also still have young in their burrows and constantly come in across the sea with a few fish in their extraordinary triangular beak, with its red, yellow and blue stripes. When they emerge, they look like large swallows as they speed away over the water. There are also fulmars sitting on the cliff ledges with their downy young among the white sea campion.

All these young birds will soon be fledged; the puffins will be back in the Atlantic and the skuas off the African coasts. But in September there will be the great invasion of southbound migrants and of twitchers. It is easier to get there now that Atlantic Airways has regular, relatively inexpensive London–Shetland flights, with a short-hop flight or ferry connection to Fair Isle.

It would have been a shame not to see one rare bird while I was there, and fortunately I did. It was a lesser grey shrike from the Balkans, and it was sitting comfortably on top of a tall wild angelica plant.

The waders from the north are beginning to come in now on their way to Africa. They like a few days' rest and refreshment on British mud.

I have just had an excellent morning watching some of them on one of my favourite Essex estuaries, the Crouch. Most of them were not on the estuary shore, since the tide was almost in and lapping against the seawall, but in the sheep meadows behind the seawall there are two lakes, or 'fleets', each with a hide beside it, and from one of these I saw some good birds.

The best, because I do not see them often, was a wood sandpiper. These birds nest in the rich, flooded woods of Scandinavia and migrate south across the Continent. However, there has been a trickle of them lately through Britain, on the western fringe of their route.

On its own at a distance, it is not so easy to tell a wood sandpiper from the much more common green sandpiper. Luckily, my bird was probing on the muddy edge of the fleet just beside a green sandpiper, and the differences were plain. The green sandpiper looks very black above; the wood sandpiper is much browner in colour, with a little speckling, and is also distinctly smaller. It has a pale eye-stripe, and on this bird, at least, the white of the underparts went right up to the top of its flank, almost to the shoulder. The green sandpiper is darker all around the upper breast. These small differences count!

When they fly up, the two birds are more distinct – the green sandpiper like a large house martin with its white rump and the wood sandpiper altogether browner, though it too has a white rump. The green sandpiper makes a loud, high-pitched cry and the wood sandpiper a thinner, drier call. But on this day, these two birds stayed resolutely bobbing about on the mud.

Also along the banks were three elegant greenshanks, silvery-grey and striding about on their long, green legs. A turnstone with black gorget flew in from the estuary shore. But the most beautiful birds of the morning were six tall, black-tailed godwits, still in their summer plumage with an exquisite pink neck and breast. The length of their beak – three times the width of their head – never fails to astonish me, however often I see it. They are eager feeders, though, and most of the time both head and beak were underwater. These birds had probably come from Iceland. Some of them may stay around all winter – but their pink will fade away.

I have been in some beautiful, unspoilt farming country in south Warwickshire. The pale-brown wheat was almost ready to be cut, its ears lolling at the top of the stalks, and as I walked along a lane in the early morning sunshine I heard three yellowhammers singing.

Almost all the other birds are silent now apart from cooing woodpigeons, but yellowhammers go on nesting and singing into August. The first that I heard was on the branch of a small, dead elm in a hedge. It is a little-known fact that there are still elms in our hedges – but they never reach more than fifteen or twenty feet and then they die. At least they provide perches for birds.

This yellowhammer had a perfect sulphur-yellow head and throat, but otherwise looked a bit dishevelled, perhaps after a summer bringing up its young. It was only singing the 'chink, chink, chink' opening of its song, not the 'cheese' at the end. But it was a bold bird and let me walk past without breaking off singing.

The next yellowhammer was a few hundred yards down the lane, singing on top of a hawthorn tree in the hedge. This one was delivering the whole 'little bit of bread and no *cheese*' song in full. The third bird I did not see, since rather unusually it was singing inside the hedge, just as a skulking whitethroat might. But I put my ear to the hedge and heard the ringing notes and the wheezing conclusion very clearly. All these singing male yellowhammers may well have had a mate sitting on a nest nearby in the hedge, but if so all of them sat tight.

Yellowhammers have gone down in numbers in recent years, so it was cheering to see these three birds so close to each other. A recent experiment in Scotland by the British Trust for Ornithology has indicated that there may be a fresh way of helping them. Farmers nowadays are encouraged to leave good margins round their fields where birds can find seeds and insects, but in late summer yellowhammers seem to find the grass too long. However, when open patches were cut in these margins the local yellowhammers readily came down to them to feed.

Robin

In the lane, there was one more surprise for me. Just past the third yellowhammer, I suddenly heard a burst of sweeter song from the hedge. It was a robin singing. Robins have been silent for the past month. So I heard the last of the summer songs and the first of the autumn songs side by side.

The soft 'chup, chup' calls of long-tailed tits can be heard again after their summer silence. Watch and you'll see several of them flitting from one tree to the next, like little teaspoons dancing through the air. They do not stay long in one place, just hanging for a moment on a leafy twig to pick up an insect, before setting off on their way again.

These small groups are mainly family flocks. The nucleus is the breeding pair and their eight or nine offspring, but there are usually a few others, often the uncles and aunts of the young ones, who hung around with the breeding pair in spring, but did not nest themselves.

The flock moves steadily on. But it will come back again, for the family and its hangers-on hold a large communal territory of woods and gardens during the winter. They work their way round and round their patch, keeping other flocks out. Being in a flock is of great benefit to them: on an icy night they huddle together to keep warm. But towards the end of the winter, the young females change camps, leaving their family to join rival flocks. Here they can find a male without risk of inbreeding.

In early spring the flocks break up and the couples, new and old, build their extraordinary nests in gorse bushes, thick hedges or tree forks. These domed structures with a hole at the side for entrance take a long time to build and are woven from grass and moss, camouflaged with lichen, bound in a net of spiders' webs and lined with 1,000 or more feathers.

Inside, the female lays a large clutch of eggs, and the pair will have many mouths to feed when these hatch. Once again, there are a few aunts and uncles around to help the nesting pair to feed their brood.

It was thought that many long-tailed tits must have died in last winter's cold spell. However, it is becoming clear that a great many managed to survive. Now these delightful little black-and-white birds with their rosy flush are beginning their rounds once more.

I have just heard robins singing again for the first time since early July. There were two of them, one on each side of the railway station at Bayford in Hertfordshire. The railway line was obviously the boundary between their two territories, and each was singing to tell the other not to cross it.

Robins have been moulting over the past month and when they are doing that they keep quiet, because without a full set of feathers, especially wing feathers, they are not so good at escaping predators, whether sparrowhawks or cats. Now, though, we are about to see a furious territory war erupt. The old males are reasserting claims to the territories they held in the summer. But they are suddenly faced with a host of competitors. Many female robins take up their own territories in the autumn, and they may find themselves in competition with their old partner. There is also a flood of speckled, young robins who want a territory too. So as August goes on, and well into September, we shall hear a chorus of song duels between these birds. The female robins are now singing just like the males. There will also be fights, some of them fierce, and there will be dead robins on the ground before autumn.

But by October the serious boundary quarrels will be over. But for the rest of the winter every territory-owning robin will go on singing, warning all others to keep out of the territory that it has been tacitly granted. If one comes near, it will be chased away. In fact, robins will get angry about even a tuft of robin's red breast feathers hanging on a stick in their territory, as the great robin expert the late Dr David Lack demonstrated. Another ornithologist, Chris Mead, claimed that robins would attack his red beard.

We are lucky that this is the robin's way of life, since it means that on cold winter days when no other bird is singing we still hear the robin's song – a sharp burst, followed by a sweet, trickling afterthought that fades away, sometimes with a touch of sadness in it. In well-lit town gardens one can even hear robins singing in the middle of the long nights.

It was a peaceful scene. There were three doves sitting quietly in the sunshine on a dried-up stretch of marsh and a little egret stalking slowly along behind them where the ground was a bit damper. Occasionally, the egret's quiff lifted in the breeze.

Then, suddenly, the three doves flew up, alarmed. However, there was nothing to alarm them – only another of the doves coming in. They circled round and landed again with the new arrival.

These were stock doves, which are smaller, not-so-well-known relatives of the woodpigeon. They look quite like hawks in the air, and what I had seen was something that I had only read about before – namely that they will sometimes mistake one of their own species for a raptor.

One reason why these birds are unfamiliar is that in the woods they are very shy, darting away before you can get more than a glimpse of them. However, they come out into the fields to feed and these resting birds are easy to recognise.

Stock Dove

Stock doves lack the white neck bar of the woodpigeon, but that is not an infallible way of identifying them because young woodpigeons lack it too. However, they are a more bluish tint of grey and the tips of their wings and the end of their tail are black, so on the ground they look noticeably black at the rear.

In the air they are also distinctive. The centre of their wings is bluish, surrounded by a dark margin, and they have a pale-blue rump, while they lack the woodpigeon's white wing bars. The oddest thing about them is their song. It is about the worst song of any British bird, being no more than a grunt followed by a sigh – 'woo-woot, woo … woot'.

Stock doves nest in holes in trees – the 'stock' in their name means tree trunk – and they seem like comfortable, peaceful birds. But the male has one aggressive trait. In spring, when his mate is fertile, he will not allow her any rest. He chases her about everywhere because he does not want her to have a moment to meet other males. Most male birds try to guard their mates during that season. But the stock dove seems the most jealous of them all.

An odd little bird that used to be called the fan-tailed warbler may be found nesting in Britain soon. It is creeping up the west coast of France and one or two have already been seen on the Channel Islands and in Kent.

It lives in wet, rushy ditches in farmland, where it can be seen putting on a strange performance. It bounces up and down in the air, as if on a string, flapping its wings wildly, fanning its tail and making a sharp 'zit' call. In Egypt, I used to watch dozens of them doing this beside the Sweet Water Canal that runs beside the Suez Canal.

Recently, the fan-tailed warbler has been given a bizarre change of name, becoming the 'zitting cisticola' – cisticola being the name of the genus to which it belongs and zitting, obviously, denoting its call. British birdwatchers dislike this absurd name and I have noticed 'fan-tailed warbler' making a comeback in many publications.

British holidaymakers going to the Dordogne in southern France can now find out exactly where they have a chance of seeing this little bird. A guide, called *Birding Dordogne*, has just been published. Its author, David Simpson, lives in the region and has tracked down all the birds of that lovely, walnut-shaded countryside.

But the fan-tailed warbler (I, too, will fight back over the name) is only one of many fascinating species, rare or unknown in Britain, that Simpson locates. Others include the booted eagle, the paler, grander short-toed eagle, the crested lark, the ortolan bunting and the woodchat shrike.

There are five species of woodpecker listed. Besides our own green woodpecker and the great and lesser spotted woodpeckers, Simpson has found that mysterious in-between bird the middle spotted woodpecker, and the dramatic, grotesque-looking black woodpecker, a recent arrival in the Dordogne.

For holidaymakers who do not want to do any energetic exploring, *Birding Dordogne* has 'the classic rural French mix of hoopoe, golden oriole, serin, cirl bunting and black redstart, which can be found in or around almost any small village'. What a thought!

Red kites are noisy this month. There are many of them nowadays in the Chiltern Hills, the place where they were first reintroduced in 1989, but generally they are silent as they glide over the valleys, scarcely moving their wings and steering themselves on the wind by a twist this way and that with their forked tails.

Red Kite

Now, however, they have young birds hiding in the beech woods, and when I was in the Chilterns last weekend I heard plenty of sound from them. Their usual call, when they have occasion to utter it, is a loud, sharp 'whee-oo', but coming from deep in the treetops I heard a longer version of this. After the sharp sound there came a little trickle of softer 'oo's, which made the call much more musical. When families are together, red kites evidently choose to sing, though it is not known why.

There was a great deal of hostility towards red kites among farmers when they were first let loose, for fear that they would kill lambs. However, in the Chilterns it has now been accepted that they feed mainly on carrion, not live creatures, with the exception of frogs. A friend of mine often sees one swoop down over the banks of his pond to pick one up.

Unlike the Chilterns' inhabitants, crows still hate kites and are always attacking them. The kite just sails away on its powerful wings. Buzzards are more often seen with them in the sky nowadays, and there is a rumour that these have been introduced deliberately to help the kites. Buzzards feed mainly on rabbits and often leave some remains on the ground. These, it is said, provide a supply of carrion for the kites. It would be an ingenious ploy by conservationists, but I have found no evidence that it is true.

In various other places where red kites have been reintroduced, they have had a harder time, especially in Scotland, where many are still poisoned. Overall, though, the experiment of bringing them back to Britain, where they were once found even in London, has been a marked success. It is unfailingly exciting to see one coming over-head, with its five-foot wingspan, its ruddy plumage gleaming in the sun and its orange tail waggling.

One of those curious chants that used to be heard from soldiers lazing on their beds in army barrack rooms goes: 'A man put his hand in a woodpecker's hole. The woodpecker said "Cor, bless my soul! Take it out! Take it out! Remove it!"'

It is true that woodpeckers nest in holes, but, apart from that, green woodpeckers spend most of their time on the ground. They may pick the odd bug out of the bark on a tree trunk, but their main food is ants.

At present their loud, laughing cries can be heard ringing through the woods, breaking the deep August woodland silence, because they are still looking after their young in the trees. But, after that, they will be out of the woods and hunting for anthills.

They are not difficult to watch when they are feeding on an anthill on a bumpy hillside, if you creep up cautiously. They are splendid-looking birds with their varied green body, black face and long, red crown. The male sports a black and red moustache, the female a plain black one.

Their tongue is their main instrument for catching ants. It can be extended to about five inches long and is very sticky, so it can sweep through a crowd of agitated ants on the grass or earth and pick them and their white pupae up at the same time. If the anthill lies under a thick layer of turf, the woodpecker plunges its beak in and makes a deep hole. The ants fall off the side of the hole and the woodpecker's tongue catches them as they drop. If you find a little mound full of gashes in a field, you know that it is an anthill that has received a green woodpecker's attention.

When they fly up, they make a more excited version of their mellow summer laugh and, as they undulate away, all that the eye usually takes in is the brilliant golden patch gleaming on their lower back. In the trees, they move to the far side of the trunk when you approach, and if you follow them round, they spiral up and up the trunk. It is a good game then to see if you can go round fast enough to catch up with them.

There are not many red-billed choughs (pronounced 'chuffs') in Britain, but with luck you can see some as you sit outside a cafe, with a crab sandwich or cream tea in front of you, at the southernmost point of the Lizard peninsula in Cornwall. The Royal Society for the Protection of Birds has a telescope there, through which you can often watch them swirling round the caves where they nest.

Choughs are lively, black birds, not unlike their relatives the jackdaws but with a long, sharp red beak and a way of flying with their wing feathers well spread. They became extinct in Cornwall in 1947. But in 2001 three suddenly appeared on the Lizard Peninsula. The RSPB, along with Natural England and the National Trust, set out to protect them, and in 2011 there were six pairs along this stretch of the Cornish coast, while fifteen young birds fledged successfully.

Management of the choughs has consisted mainly of providing plenty of areas with short grass for them to feed on along the cliff tops, since they do not thrive without that. Grazing by livestock, as well as by rabbits, is what the grass needs. This has required cooperation with local landowners and farmers, which has been very successful. One paradox is that tourists give considerable help to the choughs by regularly walking and sitting on the grass, though at the same time they may disturb them. The tourist balance seems, on the whole, favourable to the birds. There is also 24-hour protection of the nests against egg collectors by teams of volunteers.

There are a few other places along the west coasts of Britain and Ireland where choughs can be seen, notably on the Hebridean island of Islay. There are also some in Brittany. But the Cornish restoration is a real triumph. I have a canvas book-bag produced by Cornwall Council with a picture of the bird and a pile of books on it, and the legend: 'Choughed with libraries.' They really love their choughs down in Cornwall.

September

In the pretty village of Great Chesterford near Cambridge there was one bird call that rang out through the silence of the morning. This was the call of the greenfinch. It was not their wheezing spring call, nor their rollicking song, but the impatient 'choo, choo' that they make when they are feeding in the trees.

The greenfinches had come into the yew trees in the churchyard and gardens to feed on the new pink berries. They like these for the sweet, juicy flesh that encases the hard seed inside. Other birds like them too, and I saw a song thrush slipping through the dark-green branches of one tree in search of them. The seeds themselves are very poisonous, but they pass through the birds and find their way to fresh ground, which is exactly what the trees want. The seeds are coated with a substance that resists digestive juices, which makes the whole process even easier for both parties.

I wrote in March about a throat disease called trichomonosis that has been affecting greenfinches and, as there seemed to be few greenfinches in the country around London at that time, I expressed a fear that it might have hit them there too. However, I need not have worried. Soon after, plenty of them appeared, and they have been common and noticeable all the summer.

I walked on through the hilly wheat fields that surround the village and even there they dominated the scene, insofar as any birds did. One or two tractors were at work, but they were not ploughing in the wheat stubble, with the usual flocks of rooks and gulls behind. They were sowing oilseed rape – which nowadays is done without ploughing, leaving the stubble to rot under the new crop. So the fields were bare of birds, except for the odd red-legged partridge whirring up.

However, every time I passed a little roadside cluster of houses and barns, there the greenfinches were, calling and looking for berries and seeds in the hedges and yards. With their bright green plumage and golden wing bars, they proved to be very good companions on my walk through the quiet of the countryside.

The liveliest little waders appearing around our coasts just now are the ringed plovers. Whereas the small waders with longer bills, such as dunlins, tend to go plodding steadily along, probing the mud for tiny organisms, the ringed plovers skitter about, picking up sea snails and such from the surface. I watched about twenty of them feeding on a small group of mud islands in an Essex estuary. They are instantly recognisable with their white collar and black mask.

The only other bird like them is their cousin the little ringed plover, but that is not a coastal bird. On gravel pits, where both species can be seen together, the ringed plover can be distinguished in flight by its white wing bar, while its smaller relative has plain, brown wings.

The birds I was watching were noisy as well as sprightly, with their clear 'too-ee' calls coming constantly across the water to where I was standing on the seawall. They were obliged to fly up quite a lot since the tide was coming in, and one by one the islands were being submerged. Soon they were all together on the largest, and last remaining, island.

Their feeding technique was to stand still and look for a moment, then run quickly to some morsel they had seen and pick it up by bending their whole head and body forward. Once or twice I saw one of them 'pattering' – standing on one foot while tapping the mud with the other. They do this either to attract worms up to the surface or to soften the mud so that it is easier to pull things out.

In summer, ringed plovers nest mainly on shingle, where their black-and-white head markings camouflage them against the pebbles. In recent years they have been nesting more often inland. On Fair Isle I found several pairs amid the heather above the sea cliffs. Some of the ringed plovers passing through in autumn come from Canada and Greenland and go on to West Africa. But our own ringed plovers do not go so far. Many of them spend the winter on the French or Iberian coasts, while others stay quite happily at home.

Great tits are singing again. The familiar 'teacher, teacher' song is starting to be heard in woods and gardens after three months' silence. The birds themselves are looking very spruce after their moult, and the young ones have lost their yellow cheeks in favour of clean, white ones.

They sing mainly in the early morning. After that they join up with flocks of other tits and all of them search for food together. The great tits are using their song to stake an early claim to their territory for next year, but they will not spend much time in it until after Christmas. By that time there will probably be far fewer of them.

There has been some discussion in *The Times* letters page over whether sparrowhawks and other raptors harm the populations of smaller birds. They kill and eat individuals, of course, but do they bring the numbers down?

In the case of the great tit and the sparrowhawk, the answer now seems clear. Great tit populations are cut back in winter almost entirely by a shortage of food. The dominant great tits fight if necessary to keep food for themselves, and many of the weaker ones die of starvation. All that the predatory sparrowhawks do is cream off some of the weaker great tits who would die anyway. So their impact on the population is practically nil.

There are about two million pairs of great tits breeding here in the summer and that total seems to be fairly stable. This means that a number equivalent to all the young great tits that are produced each summer dies every winter. There is room enough there for our 40,000 pairs of sparrowhawks to eat great tits if they want to!

One interesting fact emerged when sparrowhawks became rarer here thirty or forty years ago as a result of the impact of pesticides. With less need to watch out for sparrowhawks, great tits had more time to look for food and the dominant ones all became distinctly fatter. When the sparrowhawks recovered, they found it easier to catch these fat birds because they were less agile. So the dominant birds soon became leaner again.

There was an even more extraordinary consequence. The weaker, more submissive great tits tend to build up their strength in times of abundant food, as a defence against the possibility of times getting bad for them again. So these now became the fatter birds – and in consequence they, in turn, became the main prey of the sparrowhawks. Such are the strange cycles of history in the world of birds.

We hear a lot about birds that have been successfully reintroduced in Britain, but we do not hear much about a remarkable bird that since 1955 has colonised the country without any help from human beings: the collared dove.

It is an amazing story. These Balkan doves started moving west across Europe in 1930. In 1955 the first pair bred in Britain, in Kent. Now they are everywhere, even in the furthest Hebrides. You can hear them singing, quite anachronistically, in the Victorian gardens of TV films. And they are still moving out of the Balkans, currently trying to take over Russia. Has Vladimir Putin noticed?

You cannot mistake these pale doves with a pinkish face, a white-tipped tail and a black half-collar. They sing a loud song with the accent on the middle note – 'cuck-*coo*-coo' – and people hearing them sometimes think they are cuckoos. They also give a loud squawk and lift their tail when they land on roofs.

The collared dove started by colonising farmyards where there was scattered grain to feed on, but they are most common now in the semi-rural outskirts of towns and cities, often nesting in small trees in large gardens. They are often seen sitting and preening on TV aerials – in Germany they are called the 'television dove'.

In summer each pair holds a small territory around the nest, but they are not very energetic in defending it. The males display above the territory, flying up steeply and squawking as they glide down again. The pairs tend to stay together from one year to the next. Some are still nesting and will go on into October. They have several broods every year. The nests are very flimsy platforms made of sticks, and from below you can see the two white eggs gleaming through the gaps.

Doves and pigeons are alternative names for the members of one vast bird family and throughout the world they lay two eggs in each brood. On learning this fact, Naomi Lewis, the late children's writer who was well known for looking after injured birds, remarked: 'Then all the pigeons we ever see are twins!'

I heard a little owl as I was going down a lane the other day. It was on the far side of the hedge and I could not get into the field to look for it, but the call was unmistakable. It is a sharp, rather high-pitched 'ker-week' that carries a long way.

A few years ago, when buzzards were rare visitors to eastern England, I heard what I thought was a little owl, but when I looked up I was amazed to see a buzzard sailing overhead. I realised then that the little owl's call is like a brisk, soldierly version of the buzzard's drawling, languorous cry.

Little owls are often out and about hunting in daytime. They sit in pollarded willows overlooking a field, or on fences and five-barred gates. I once came across one sitting on the name board outside the entrance to a country house, about eighteen inches above the ground. It flew across several times to the grass verge on the opposite side of the road and each time picked up something, probably a beetle.

When it was on its perch it kept looking at me, bobbing nervously up and down, but it held its ground. Little owls look wonderful when they stare at you, their white eyebrows curving down in a frown and their yellow eyes gleaming in their round face. They are small birds, but they are not timid. After all, they belong to the eagle owl family, not the tawny owl family.

They feed mainly on small mammals, insects and worms. They tug worms out of the earth like a blackbird does and have been seen falling over backwards when doing this. However, they will also attack small birds, and one was recently observed flying straight into a flock of starlings and catching one of them. On such occasions little owls fly swiftly and directly, but otherwise they have an undulating flight like a woodpecker's. You see them most often lolloping away from you across a field.

They are not native British birds, though they are common on the Continent. They were deliberately introduced here by various landowners between the late nineteenth century and 1930. But they have thrived here, with between 5,000 and 10,000 pairs now nesting in Britain, and I am very glad indeed that they have been so successful.

Black redstarts have been turning up, on migration, on various tall buildings – among them Sizewell B power station, near Leiston, in Suffolk. The males are dashing little birds, practically all black, with bright red, quivering tails. The brown female also has the tail. Among Britons, they are best known to holidaymakers in Continental cities, where they nest on roofs. In Avignon once, I opened the window of my hotel room to look at the Papal palace in the distance, but the first thing I saw was a black redstart singing just in front of me. Their song is a brisk warble with a sinister buzzing note in it. You often hear it, look up, and see the singer's tail disappearing behind a crocket on a church roof.

Black Redstart

A few pairs breed in Britain, and that is an interesting story. In 1942 they invaded London and started nesting in the ruins of bombed-out buildings, where, on the blackened ground beneath, the newly arrived pink flowers of rosebay willowherb were rampaging. They were originally birds of mountain and sea cliffs, and buildings have provided a new range of nest sites for them. They have continued to breed in Britain, including London. I have matched one from platform 11a at King's Cross railway station. A pair has also nested on the O2 arena, in Greenwich, south-east London.

Their numbers had shot up to about 100 pairs, but have declined again, and about fifty pairs are thought to be here each summer. Some are in London, though you never know what buildings they will choose. There are also a few pairs in other counties of England, including a pair that has nested in the city centre in Manchester, with the male singing above the heads of the shoppers. In Sussex, they have reverted to their ancestral habitat, with nests spotted on inaccessible cliffs.

The best way to find one in summer is to listen for its song. There is not much birdsong coming down from city roofs and though the traffic may be noisy, the black redstart's song comes down loud and clear in the gaps. I once heard one singing on top of the Indian YMCA in Central London. What a pleasant surprise it was!

Wigeon from Iceland and Scandinavia are beginning to appear on our lakes and estuaries. During the summer, there are only about 400 pairs of this delightful duck here, making their nests under the bracken and heather on the shores of Scottish lochs. But by January there will be nearly half a million wigeon in Britain.

These first arrivals sometimes look rather weird and patchy, with many of the old drakes still coming out of their dull 'eclipse' plumage and the young drakes emerging from their juvenile plumage. But once the drakes are in their new, bright feathers they are beautiful and unmistakable birds.

Wigeons have a round, chestnut-coloured head, with a butter-coloured forehead that can look creamy white when the low sun shines straight onto it. Their breast is a pale pink and most of the rest of their body is a delicately speckled grey. A white stripe on their wing can also usually be seen when they swim or walk about.

The females are not so instantly distinguishable from female mallards or gadwall, though their mottled brown plumage has a reddish hint about it. Their shape is what best picks them out – the round head, the relatively short bill, the hunched posture and the little pointed tail.

They belong to the group of surface-feeding ducks and can be seen dabbling in shallow water and upending. Like gadwall, they will also hang around upending mute and whooper swans and diving coots to pick up any underwater vegetation that these may scatter when they come up.

However, wigeon also feed onshore more than any other British duck does. They are grazing birds, and large flocks will waddle across waterside fields, snipping and pulling up grass as they go with their strong jaws. They often fly into fields to eat like this on nights when the moon is full.

Brent geese, which will be coming here soon from Siberia, also spend much time feeding in fields like this and the wigeon frequently graze alongside them.

In spite of their charming looks and ways, perhaps the most memorable thing about wigeon is the drakes' call. It is a loud, echoing 'whee-ooo' and can be heard from the flocks at any time when they are on the water. It is especially haunting when it comes ringing out of the mist shrouding a lake or estuary at dawn, and not a bird can yet be seen. That is a powerful memory that often comes to the mind of wildfowlers, fishermen and early-morning walkers.

I was crossing some hilly farmland in Hertfordshire earlier this week, and as I came over the crest of one field I saw a large flock of gulls in a newly harrowed field on the other side of the valley in front of me. They were not, as I had first imagined, black-headed gulls, but proved to be the much larger lesser black-backed species, with only two or three black-headed gulls tagging along with them.

There were just over sixty of them, mostly adults, with a few dark-brown, younger birds, and they were a handsome sight. Lesser black-backs have a slate-coloured back that contrasts sharply with their shining white head and underparts, and they are more elegant than the stout and solid-looking herring gulls, who are their closest relatives. They are slimmer, and their wings are a little longer and narrower. One or two were flying about and I could see how deftly they turned in the air. For the most part, though, they stood around not doing much.

Lesser Black-Backed Gull

These gulls were migrants from further north, no doubt, and a few years ago I would have supposed they were on their way to the Mediterranean. It was unusual in the past for any of them to spend the winter here. Now, however, many of them remain in Britain for the colder months, and perhaps these birds were not intending to go much further. They eat fish, of course, and in summer will kill birds such as puffins. In winter, however, they regularly forage inland, eating worms and even voles in the fields.

More than 100,000 pairs nest here in the summer, some on shingle and sand dunes along the coast and many on the Scottish moors and in the Pennines. They have also taken to nesting on rooftops, especially in Gloucester, where they are regarded as a great nuisance. They can be fierce, even coming down and chasing dogs.

But one of the most remarkable colonies I have seen

is on the long, shingly peninsula of Orford Ness on the Suffolk coast, now owned by the National Trust. Here, beside the ruins of the huts in which radar was developed during the 1930s, about 6,000 of them sit on nests all over the ground. Even here they are not very welcome, because they are sitting on a unique shingle heath of lichens and mosses and their nests of seaweed and the other mess that they deposit do not help the habitat. Nevertheless, a boat trip to the Ness in summer offers bird lovers a really remarkable spectacle.

A friend of mine with a country house in Oxfordshire once said to me: 'When I start pouring drinks at my party tonight, if you look through the French windows you'll see a barn owl fly past along the hedge at the end of the garden.'

He was right. As he popped the first champagne cork, a gleaming white figure floated along beside the hedge and disappeared into the dusk.

Barn owls come out at sunset to start hunting and go on till dawn. They like to fly beside hedges because they hope to find plenty of shrews and mice in the rough grass below. This makes country lanes very attractive to them. But it also puts them in danger because many, especially the young ones, are killed by cars on the road.

Barn Owl

As an example, the Hawk and Owl Trust has found that from October 2010 to March 2011, seventy-three dead barn owls were picked up on the roads of Norfolk alone. A sad figure. Now the trust is trying to set up a scheme to protect them. It has invented a device – a high-tech sensor – that will alert the owls to an approaching car. Positioned in a hedge, it will emit a sharp sound as soon as car headlights appear on the road 100 yards away. It is hoped that this will frighten off the owls. There will actually be five different sounds on the sensor and they will be activated randomly, so that the owls do not get used to a particular sound.

A similar device has been used successfully to scare elks

off the roads at night in Sweden – though the Swedes are more concerned about human deaths in a collision than about elk casualties. The problem in Britain has been finding the places where barn owls repeatedly hunt at night. Nigel Middleton, the trust's conservation officer for East Anglia, has been plotting the sites of known barn owl deaths in Norfolk on a map, but says that no pattern has yet emerged to show where it would be best to try out the device.

If you come across a dead barn owl, or hit one, in Norfolk the trust would be glad to hear where (www.hawkandowl.org).

<u>October</u>

Three kinds of tiny bird are now battling across the sea to get to Britain. They are goldcrests, firecrests and yellow-browed warblers.

British goldcrests – of which there are getting on for a million pairs – stay at home for the winter, but Scandinavian goldcrests migrate here in October, sometimes in quite large numbers. Firecrests breed all over the Continent, and a few also nest here in the summer, but we generally get a small winter invasion, too, and there has been a distinct trickle of them this week, especially into Norfolk.

Goldcrests and firecrests live much the same kind of lives, restlessly searching for tiny insects, hanging under the needles of conifers or hovering over them, or tracking steadily along the twigs at the bottom of a hedge.

They are both little greenish birds that would hardly be noticeable if it were not for their heads. But what heads! Goldcrests have a black line above each eye and in the middle a flaming crest. The males are particularly striking, with a bright orange crest that becomes more yellow at the front. Firecrests are exactly the opposite. The male's crest is yellow at the back and such a vivid orange at the front that it produces a kind of fire-flash when the bird turns its head. Altogether the firecrest's head is more dramatic than the goldcrest's, since it has a dark line through the eye, a white stripe above that and a dark line bordering the crest on each side.

Goldcrest

But now another difficulty has loomed if one is trying to distinguish between these birds. Yellow-browed warblers from Siberia have started invading Britain every autumn. They are busy little green birds, very like the other two and only a scrap larger.

The yellow-browed warbler lacks the bright crest – but that is not always obvious on the other two, anyway. They have a black line through the eye and a conspicuous yellowish stripe above it. All three of these species have a pair of wing bars, but they are much more pronounced in the yellow-browed warbler and its wings have a generally rather creamy look. It has a sharp call like a coal tit's.

With a good view, all these features should make it fairly easy to pick out a yellow-browed warbler – but, as all birdwatchers know, in nature it is rarely as simple as that. One last clue – yellow-browed warblers like sycamore trees!

If it really took a white stork to bring us a baby, Britain would be depopulated. The last white storks to nest in Britain were a pair on St Giles' Cathedral in Edinburgh in 1416. A few white storks always pay us a visit in autumn, however – birds that have drifted off their migration route from central Europe to Gibraltar and on to Africa. One has been touring around Kent, another round Sussex and, most recently, one in Dorset.

It is a startling moment for us Britons when a stork comes swooping out of the sky and lands among sheep or horses in a meadow. They are very tall, white birds with a black rear, a long red beak and red legs. They plod about looking for frogs and grasshoppers and when they fly up again, they do not rest their head on their shoulders like a heron, but stretch their long necks out in front of them.

We have never had much of a chance to get fond of them, but on the Continent they are hailed with joy when they come back each spring. People put up cart wheels on tall poles or platforms on roofs to give them somewhere to nest – a pair on a house is thought to bring it good luck.

They build huge nests of sticks and mud and decorate them with miscellaneous bits of plastic. But they are noisy birds to have living upstairs. The male and female greet each other at the nest by making a loud clattering with their beaks.

Most British people associate storks with Holland, but that is no longer justified. There are only about a dozen pairs left there now. On our side of Europe, the best place to see them is Spain, where you find them in fields among the cork oak trees.

The great European country for them, however, is Poland, where more than 40,000 pairs nest. Nevertheless, there is always a chance of seeing one in Britain. They are most frequent in the south – but one has been seen on a lamp-post in Manchester and another on a cricket pitch in Angus.

Black kites are probably the most abundant raptors in the world, scavenging on long, elegant wings in streets and harbours right across the south of Europe, Africa, southern Asia and Australia. In Britain they are rare visitors, though up to three have been flying about in Cornwall and one was reported over the Hog's Back in Surrey. They are similar to the red kites that are now familiar in many parts of this country after their reintroduction, but black kites look darker in the sky and have a tail that is much less deeply forked than the red kite's.

I have been watching them on the shores of Lake Como, where they swoop over the lakeside promenades of towns such as Bellagio, picking up dead fish in the water, then soaring back into the hills.

One morning I saw an arresting Italian version of what is now a common British scene. In Britain carrion crows, which are our ordinary crows, often try to attack red kites. In Italy the crows are hooded crows. These are close relatives of the carrion crow and were once considered just a subspecies of it, but are now adjudged to be a full species. They have grey bodies with a pink tinge in the sunlight, black wings and tail, and a black hood. They are the crows of central and eastern Europe, but there is a strange isolated community of them in north-west Scotland, and they are also the crow of Ireland.

I was watching a black kite fly alongside the high, grey crags above the lake when suddenly two hooded crows rose from a pylon and tried to attack it. It glided nonchalantly away, easily outpacing them. I noticed how straight it kept its wings, so that as it disappeared it looked like no more than a thin pencil line in the sky.

For me, this suddenly felt like a dream version of a familiar experience – not black crows chasing a sturdy red kite across the green slopes of the Chilterns, but odd pinkish crows with an executioner's hood pursuing a skeletal black kite beside Alpine peaks. I have been remembering it frequently in recent days – and it still seems quite surreal.

I was looking at the sunlight playing on a large yew tree, which was making the red berries gleam, when suddenly a nuthatch darted into the branches. It went to the end of a twig, picked a berry with its beak and shot off with it.

This is not the sort of scenario in which you would normally see a nuthatch. This small, blue bird, with white underparts and a black line across the eye, is more often found in the branches of the treetops. It can walk upon every part of a tree with its sturdy legs and grasping claws – it can even go head first down the trunk. It likes yew berries, but its main diet in the autumn and winter is nuts.

At this time of the year the nuthatch is the great 'tapper' in the trees. That morning, as I continued to walk through the woods, I kept hearing tap-tapping sounds. I knew that it was nuthatches. They had found a hazelnut or an early acorn, wedged it into a crack in the bark of the tree and were now hammering at the shell to get at the kernel.

There are other birds that make tapping noises. Great spotted woodpeckers bang away at bark to get at insects behind it; marsh tits make an extraordinary amount of noise, pecking at rotten tree stumps for the same purpose. But at this time of year it is the nuthatches that lead the tapping chorus.

They also have a distinctive call, which is now ringing out in the woods. This is a rapid succession of slightly slurred whistles, very much like the sound made by a stone skimmed across a frozen lake as it skips over the ice.

At nesting time nuthatches are notable tree trunk walkers. They will also build a mud wall across the entrance of a suitable nesting cavity, then – by going in and out of it repeatedly before it dries – make a round hole that is their size exactly, thus keeping out the starlings and woodpeckers.

Meanwhile, they are not only eating nuts but also hiding them in the ground, like jays and squirrels. On winter days they will unearth them – and, if they have stored enough of them, the tap-tapping will continue into the spring.

Nuthatch

An agreeable sound just now is the song of the starlings in late afternoon. They gather on high perches and chatter, whirr and whistle together in little relaxed groups. The song comes down from treetops, transmission masts and even the top of electricity pylons.

Sometimes a familiar sound from elsewhere mingles with the music – the sound of a burglar alarm, a curlew, a baby crying. Starlings are great imitators. We shall soon get a report of one imitating some strange chimes on a mobile phone. Mozart's Piano Concerto in G major (K453) has a passage in it that mimics the song of a starling that he owned (he copied the song down), but whether the bird imitated Mozart or Mozart imitated the bird is in dispute.

Why starlings sing together like this on autumn evenings is not known. It sounds very like a genial human sing-song, but perhaps there is an aggressive element to the song, with each bird warning the ones around it not to come too close.

At this time of year the look of starlings puzzles some people. From a distance they still look black, but in fact in their autumn plumage they are very speckled, with buff-ish marks like arrowheads, and they can be mistaken for some quite different, mysterious species.

Towards dusk, the singing groups take wing. They are off to their roosts, where they frequently gather in vast numbers. The small flocks link up with each other, and the nearer the roost, the larger the flocks sweeping across the sky.

However, some starlings linger around their territories from time to time in winter, and I have seen a starling on a chimney pot singing and waving its wings fiercely at an enormous flock that was passing overhead – a real little David with a sling. No doubt it flew up and joined one of the flocks eventually.

At the roosts, usually in dense woods or reed beds, the starlings give a spectacular performance. They fly around for quite a long time before settling, and the great flocks close up into giant thunderclouds, then open out into long lines like rippling, black silk in the sky. They do this again and again before all finally streaming down into the roost.

Starlings used to perform like this in the West End of London, spending the night on the ledges of tall buildings. The authorities hated the mess they left behind, but they were a wonderful sight. However, in recent years starling numbers have gone down heavily in Britain and that London spectacle takes place no more.

Last week I went to the Wetland Centre in Barnes, south-west London, in the hope of seeing a spotted crake that had been paddling about there in a reed bed. The Wetland Centre is an extraordinary place: an extensive area of pools and grazing marsh on the site of some old reservoirs, with the Knightsbridge skyline visible in the distance. Birds such as redshanks and reed warblers nest there, and many migrant birds flying over London come down to rest within its boundaries.

Spotted Crake

The spotted crake was one of these, and it had evidently liked what it found. It had already been there for a month, always lurking in about 100 yards' length of reed bed, and occasionally coming out.

It was a fresh, sunny morning, just the sort of morning when migrants take it into their head to move on, so I thought, 'It'll be just my luck to be a day too late.' However, when I got to where the crake had conveniently settled, I was assured by one of the watchers in the hide opposite that it had already been out but had been chased back into the reeds by a water rail.

'You must look over the water,' I was told, 'at the bit of reeds between the Harrods domes.' These loomed up plainly in the distance. So I looked and looked and, having no luck, eventually decided to go and get warm in the sunshine. On another pool I found a heron also warming itself up, facing the sun with its wings half open. When I went back, sure enough, a cry went up: 'It's been out but it's gone back again.' That luck of mine.

At last, after about four hours, we suddenly saw a dumpy, little, brown bird, not much bigger than a thrush, come out and walk around in the shallow water in front of the reeds. That was our crake. Through field glasses you could see its yellow beak and the pale feathers under its cocked tail. Through a telescope you could see its brown and bluish plumage with white flecking.

Someone said, 'Rare birds aren't necessarily beautiful,' and everyone laughed. All the same, this spotted crake – a bird that breeds mainly in distant European marshes – had the strange cachet of rarity that made it a wonder to us all.

A few years ago I paid a visit to the Nene Washes in Cambridgeshire to help release some corncrake chicks into the great wilderness where it was hoped that they would return and breed.

Corncrakes used to be quite common in the hay meadows of Britain – small rusty-red birds whose creaking calls
would keep farmworkers awake at night. They still call
on summer nights in a few places in the north-west of
Scotland and the west of Ireland, but they are practically
extinct in England. They were destroyed by the change to
early mechanised cutting of the hay, which wrecked their
nests and killed them.

Release of the chicks began in earnest on the RSPB
reserve in the Washes in 2003, and I took part the following August. We had eleven streaky, bright-eyed chicks
with long legs, all ringed, in soft, white cotton bags. They
had been reared at Whipsnade Zoo and then brought up
to the reserve for acclimatisation.

We opened the bags gently one by one, and each time
a small head peered out and glanced around. A moment
later a chick shot out and ran like mad into the tangled
vegetation. Would any of these delightful birds ever be
seen again? That was the big question.

Well, a few days after I was there, two un-ringed chicks
were seen running in front of a tractor – it looked as if one
of the chicks released in 2003 had returned in 2004 and
bred, and that these were its offspring.

Since then there has been a slow recolonisation. Male
corncrakes have regularly been heard calling there. It is
virtually impossible to find their nests, but if males have
returned, females have no doubt returned too. So some of
these males have probably paired and bred.

At the same time, working with crofters, the RSPB has managed to increase the numbers in Scotland, with about 1,100 birds calling in the summer now. (They go back south of the Sahara in autumn.)

I have watched corncrakes on North Uist in the Outer Hebrides. There they lurk and call unseen in the iris beds, but if one is patient one sees them pop up their orange and grey heads from time to time. From now on, with luck, people in England will have a better chance of hearing – and even seeing – them again.

Wild swans are returning for the winter. Whooper swans from Iceland are the first, and there are already more than 1,000 of them on one of their main wintering places, the flooded wetland of the Ouse Washes on the Norfolk–Cambridgeshire border. Up to another 2,000 are expected. They will be followed by the smaller Bewick's swans from Siberia.

Whooper swans are almost as large as mute swans and have a somewhat grander appearance. Whereas mute swans generally keep their long necks curved, the whoopers hold them upright and look very proud. Another feature that distinguishes them is their black-and-yellow beak, with its straight line from forehead to tip, while the mute swan's beak is curved and orange. Also, they make a trumpeting call as they fly, where mute swans are silent – except, of course, for the rich throbbing sound of their beating wings.

The Bewick's swans – named in honour of the bird artist Thomas Bewick after his death – are distinctly shorter, and the yellow patch at the base of their beak is rounded rather than triangular. Their call is a soft yelp rather than a loud whoop.

Wintering whoopers are found in much of Scotland and all over Ireland, as well as in a few places in England. Bewick's swans mostly come to Ireland and England. The Ouse Washes are an excellent place to see them, since the great flock there is fed on grain and potatoes in front of a large hide two or three times a day. Both the RSPB and the Wetlands and Wildfowl Trust (WWT) have reserves on the Washes, and this spectacle takes place on the WWT reserve at Welney. Some evening feeds are floodlit. It is a remarkable sight as these swans, normally so wild and shy, squabble in the water over the food, while a motley collection of pochards and other duck try to get a look in. However, some visitors find the scene rather diminishing to the swans. These massive birds really look at their best when they come flighting in over the fields at sunset.

The WWT has also been satellite-tracking the journeys of some whoopers by fitting them with transmitters. They have found some of them take only eighteen hours to fly here from Iceland.

Snow buntings are arriving in Britain, mainly along the east coast. They are sometimes called snowflakes, because the males have white wings and both sexes have white underparts and a flock of them looks like a small snowstorm when it comes whirling down on to a beach.

They also nest in regions of snow and ice. Of all the European land birds they breed the furthest north, high in the Arctic Circle, and they feed like white sparrows round the homes of the Inuits. They keep the upper parts of their legs warm by fluffing out their stomach feathers to make a little jacket for them.

They build their nests in crevices in the rocks, sometimes making their homes among the colonies of Arctic seabirds. Where they live among humans, they may build in holes in houses or huts, or in things like old tin cans. Sometimes they use the feathers of ptarmigans, which are also birds of the snowy wastes, to line their nests.

I have watched them in summer in Iceland, where they are common birds. They nest on the hillsides and also come into towns.

The males, which are snowy white in summer with a black back and wing tips, have a vigorous and quite musical song. They perch on rocks and roofs, lifting their head high as they sing in the typical way of buntings, and they also perform song flights. In winter most of them come south, sometimes in large flocks.

They eat seeds washed in by the sea on to the sand, and the flocks have a distinctive way of feeding. The birds in the rear of the flock fly every so often over the birds ahead of them and land again to lead the flock, so that all the birds in turn have a chance of getting the best seeds.

This rollover method of advancing along the shore is also used by flocks of twites, which come down in winter to similar feeding places. So one might see a flock of snow buntings leapfrogging along the shore at one spot, and a flock of twites doing the same thing not far along the beach.

However, one also sees solitary snow buntings along the British coast. At Minsmere I once saw a snow bunting and a dunlin feeding beside the same small pool on the shore – a very odd-looking couple, but apparently quite happy together.

A few pairs regularly nest in Scotland, up in the Highlands among the summer snows. In some summers there may be 100 pairs. They seem to be a self-contained community, with little immigration from outside.

November

Last week I suddenly found myself watching a water rail. I had been looking down from a bank at a reed bed that had had a broad opening cut through it, its bottom now covered with bits of old reed leaf and stalk.

I changed my focus to a drake goldeneye that was diving out on the lake beyond the reeds, the first that I had seen this winter. It did indeed have bright-yellow eyes. But its most noticeable features were its dark-green head with a round white patch on its cheek and the fine barring on its side. It dived repeatedly and always came up somewhere quite different, so I got only a few glimpses of it. When I looked back at the opening there was a brownish patch on the floor. It took me a moment to realise that this patch was a quiet, but busy, water rail. It had sneaked out from the reeds to peck at the reed litter with its long, red bill.

The setting sun came out behind me and lit it up. It was a beautiful bird. Its back was a speckly brown but its flanks were barred black and white, like the goldeneye's, and its face and breast were a soft, slatey blue. An old name for the water rail is 'velvet runner', which is said in dictionaries to reflect the 'stealthy way' in which it runs, but I wonder if the name does not really allude to its lovely blue front.

Water Rail

For a long time I watched it searching – perhaps for small aquatic creatures under the litter – scarcely moving except to jerk up once or twice when something alarmed it. After that it twitched its tail and started work again.

A moorhen – distinctly larger – loomed up but did not chase it away. In fact, as the rail started moving about, the moorhen followed it, as if it were a guide to the best feeding spots. Finally, the rail made its way with wary step towards the far end of the opening, and I could see it silhouetted against the silvery water of the lake. Then it vanished into the reeds.

Water rails are more often heard than seen, because they can make extraordinary squealing cries in the reeds. But I could hardly have had a more splendid view of one than that.

Nowadays nearly all our seagulls can be found inland in winter, even the massive great black-backed gull. The only one that is a rare inland visitor, except when gales blow it into unexpected places, is the kittiwake. So it is not a particularly familiar bird. Yet it is now known that the kittiwake is the most common of British gulls, with about 400,000 pairs breeding here, and is also the common-est gull in the world, with nine million adults and nine million immature birds at the annual peak.

Even in summer, when it nests on narrow cliff ledges around most of the British Isles, it can quite easily be overlooked. It is a fairly small, white gull, with a yellow bill and black legs. It also has dark, gentle-looking eyes. It is best picked out among other gulls squalling over the sea by its stiff-winged yet buoyant flight. A new book about this attractive bird, *The Kittiwake* by John Coulson, is deeply informative, as well as lucid and readable. Coulson has spent a lifetime studying kittiwakes, mostly in north-east England. One fascinating observation is that because nesting on narrow ledges puts them in danger of falling off, they have adapted their behaviour. They build more substantial nests than other gulls, so that the eggs and young birds have a fence round them. Also, the young birds in the nest do not look out to sea to watch for their parents returning with fish, but stand facing the cliff. Even the incubating adults sit patiently looking at the cliff wall.

They are enterprising birds, too. In recent years they have started nesting on buildings. Some kittiwakes built on window ledges on the Newcastle Guildhall – and when spikes were put up to deter them, they nested on top of the spikes.

During the past month, however, the kittiwakes have been heading out into the Atlantic for the winter. Somehow they will survive the storms out there. But as early as January, the first birds will be returning – and seawatchers will again be hearing the strange 'kitti-waak' cry that gives them their name.

I have been down to the Crouch estuary in Essex to see the wintering brent geese. These amazing little geese fly here all the way from the far north of Russia, but this year they were late coming, and I wondered if they would be on the Crouch yet.

I need not have worried. I stepped into the sheep fields behind the sea wall, and immediately I could hear the geese calling from the water on the far side. It is a remarkable sound. The individual geese make deep, shaky, mumbling notes, and when there are a number of them doing it at the same time it sounds as though some enormous, creaky machine is rumbling past.

However, I did not yet go and look. Hundreds of rooks were flying about over the fields and I noticed something very peculiar. When the rooks landed in the grass between me and the low sun, its rays glanced off their shiny feathers and turned them for a moment into brilliant silver birds. You would never have thought that they were just plain old rooks.

I went on up some steps to the top of the wall – and what a sight was waiting there! The tide was out and on the edge of the great stretch of mud beside the wall there was an enormous flock of brents, all grumbling away. They were quite unmistakable with their black heads and necks, their little white half-collars and the shining white patch under the tail. I calculated that there were more than 500 of them either standing on the mud, or swimming idly in the shallow water.

Out in the estuaries they feed on a maritime flower called eelgrass, but they also eat ordinary grass, and a little further along I found another hundred in the sheep meadows, all nibbling quietly away. That was 600 brents altogether – 5 per cent of the 120,000 that winter in Britain.

Curlews were stalking about them in the fields, or flying round making their wild, trilling cries, while about forty shelduck gleamed white and black on the water on the other side. Another time I would have thought them glamorous. But today they were wholly upstaged by the brent geese and their rolling Arctic music.

There is a fine bird that has been harder to find lately, but no one has made much of a fuss. This is the mistle thrush. There was a panic a few years ago when its smaller relative, the song thrush, dropped in numbers. Song thrushes have made a good recovery, but mistle thrushes no longer fly up so regularly from playing fields and the green swards of golf courses when you pass.

They are one of the few birds of the countryside that are a foot long; very handsome, with their erect carriage, soft brown back and breast spotted like a plum pudding. When they take off they are easy to identify because their underwings are an obvious silvery white colour and they make loud churring calls.

Like song thrushes, they have a short period of song in November, laying an early claim to territories that they will take up in the new year. My ears are already on the alert for the songs of both species, and I hope I will not be disappointed as I listen for a mistle thrush this autumn. Its song is not like the joyful outburst of the song thrush, with its exultant repetitions, but it is very striking. It is like a blast of a few wild notes on a trumpet, which stops abruptly as if the singer has been shot. Then it rings out triumphantly again.

Another winter characteristic of mistle thrushes is that one, or a pair, will guard a holly tree with a rich crop of red berries and drive away all other thrushes and black-birds. It is to be their winter larder. Sometimes, however, the tree will be invaded by a flock of hungry fieldfares. They are almost as big as the mistle thrushes and may overwhelm the defenders. Recently, there was a report of a variation on this scene. A solitary mistle thrush tried to keep a flock of waxwings from robbing a rowan tree of its berries.

It chased them off on their first attempt, but in a second attack several of the waxwings managed to snatch some berries. It is an enchanting picture: the thrush surrounded by these pretty pink birds with their little swept-back crests, all trying to dodge his desperate rage.

One of the most charming bird sights is a golden plover perched on a little moorland hillock in summer. Its back gleams with brilliant gold in the sunshine and it continually looks around in a very alert fashion. I once walked across miles of treeless hillside in Iceland, struggling to cross streams in deep cuttings, with only golden plovers to keep me company. They were solitary and widely separated, and as I passed each one it made a plaintive whistle, as if it were a stationmaster passing me on to the next one.

Golden Plover

As winter comes they seem very different birds. Some have come down from our own moors, and others from Iceland have joined them. They are to be found in flocks haunting mud islands in the estuaries, or on ploughland and pasture. Their backs are no longer the spangled gold that they were, but are a yellow-brown that camouflages them well. You have to look hard to make them out.

In the fields there are often lapwings with them, and sometimes there are also predatory black-headed gulls, each marking a lapwing or golden plover like a football player to try to snatch any worm that it finds. If they are disturbed they all fly up together, the gulls cutting away and the lapwings and golden plovers assembling in one flock at first. Then something quite dramatic happens. The lapwings go flopping along steadily on their rounded black-and-white wings, but all the golden plovers shoot up on their narrow wings and form a tight flock high in the sky. They fly fast and have soon swept out of sight, while the lapwings are still swirling about in a muddled way.

Lapwings are also plovers and are sometimes called green plovers. However, it is probably the golden plovers that gave the group its name. It means 'rain bird', as is more clearly seen in the French *pluvier,* from *pluie* or rain. The myth used to be that they were birds that predicted wet weather. Most probably they just got the name because they arrived in the fields at the same time as autumn rainstorms – in the days when those always came.

A few swallows have been seen during the winter in Britain in recent years, and some people have attributed this to global warming. But that is not necessarily the case. The odd swallow was seen in Britain in most winters in the twentieth century, usually flying around in the relatively mild south-west.

Swallow

However, global warming may be having some effect on swallows, and the situation has been surveyed in an article by Angela Turner in *British Birds* magazine.

One of the most striking changes is a possible increase in the length of the long tail streamers in male swallows. This is because long-tailed male swallows have been shown to have a good immune system and be more resistant to the attacks of lice. Female swallows choose them as mates in preference to males with shorter tails. It is a reflection of their health.

Now swallows have to cross the Sahara to get back to Europe to breed in the spring, after which they are often in poor condition, with low fat reserves. Moreover, the desert is currently growing larger. The swallows usually recover by feeding on insects along the north coast of Africa, such as in Algeria, where there can be a relative abundance of vegetation and of the insects found around it.

The serious change in the past twenty years has been that there is less vegetation now in the extreme north of Africa, and consequently that there are fewer insects for the exhausted swallows to eat. In these circumstances, the healthier swallows are more likely to survive – which is likely to mean the long-tailed birds among the males. Researchers in Denmark have found that the average length of the tails of male swallows in their country increased by several millimetres between 1984 and 2004. If the decline in vegetation in North Africa is due to global warming, then it seems that we can say that global warming is producing longer tails in male swallows.

Swallows that get here have been arriving earlier, and this appears to correlate with warmer springs in Britain. However, early arrival is not necessarily harmful to them. It means that they can take more time to recover before breeding, with females laying larger clutches of eggs and even having more broods in the summer. In the east of Britain, with the decline of cattle pasture and of the abundance of insects that goes with it, there are fewer swallows nowadays. But in the cattle-rich west their numbers have slightly increased in the past decade.

After the plump curlews, black-tailed godwits are our next largest waders. Twitchers call them 'blackwits'. They have very long legs, and wade far out in the water. They thrust their head and neck right beneath the surface, and since their beaks are also extremely long, this means that they can forage for water snails and shrimps deep down in lakes or in the sea. Their beaks are the opposite of curlews', since they turn up towards the tip, whereas the curlew's beak curves steadily downward.

I have often watched them on the Crouch estuary in Essex, where they are found at the sea's edge when the tide is out, or else at the small lakes or 'flashes' in the meadows behind the sea wall. For a hundred years or more they were rare birds in Britain, but in recent years they have been coming here from the Icelandic meadows in good numbers in autumn. Large flocks can be seen at present. In summer, they are spectacular birds, with an orange-red neck and breast, and tiger-like stripes on the stomach. Some of them are still in this plumage, and a flock of them standing on the shore makes you think of a brass band in ceremonial dress.

Before their nineteenth-century decline, they appear to have bred widely in our marshes, and were also much eaten. The seventeenth-century doctor, Sir Thomas Browne, said that they were 'the daintiest dish in Britain' and that they were very expensive. After their long absence, a pair nested in 1952 in the Ouse Washes on the Norfolk–Cambridgeshire border, which is a vast and lonely stretch of wetland, now famous for its wild swans in winter. Since then, they have nested here and there in such places as the Nene Washes and the Somerset Levels.

The bar-tailed godwit, a slightly smaller bird of the High Arctic, also winters on our coasts. The two species are accurately distinguished by their names. Both show a white patch at the base of the tail, but the end of the smaller bird's tail is lightly streaked, while the end of the larger bird's is black. The black-tailed godwit also has a bold, white wing bar.

It's all very well lamenting the decline in numbers of house sparrows – but what about the loss of the tree sparrows?

No one ever noticed them very much, so no one has cared so much about them. Yet between 1970 and 2006 there was an astonishing 93 per cent fall in the numbers of this delightful little bird in our countryside.

In fact, no one realised that they were a different species from the house sparrow until 1713. But it is really quite easy to distinguish them. Whereas the cap of the cock house sparrow is grey at the top, the tree sparrow's whole cap is a bright chestnut, and has given it the name 'copper head' in the north of England. The tree sparrow also has a neat, intensely black bib, while the house sparrow's bib just looks as if it has spilt something messily down its front. The sexes are alike in the tree sparrow, and a further distinguishing mark they have is a black patch, like a little mutton-chop whisker, on their white cheeks.

However, it is not surprising that they are relatively unknown, since they have always been elusive country birds, chirping away much like house sparrows on the far side of a hedge. They nest in tree holes or other rural crevices, usually in small colonies that stay in one place for a few years. Then they all move off together to somewhere new. They make an unmistakable, sharp 'tack-tack' call as they fly, and in the past I often heard them passing over a country house, and knew at once what they were.

Why they have dwindled away no one knows, though the general supposition is that they have not been able to find enough insect food for their nestlings, the apparent cause of decline in other farmland birds. But why such a dramatic fall? One suggestion is that they have proved easy prey for sparrowhawks as these raptors have recovered their numbers.

A slight increase in the tree sparrow population in the past two or three years may have been helped by the provision of nest boxes. I have watched a colony squabbling noisily at the RSPB reserve on the Ouse Washes, and another at the bird reserve on Rutland Water, where they have started coming on to the shore to feed.

What are the owls doing on these long winter nights? Tawny owls are quite happy. They have no difficulty hunting in the dark. Their ears are so sharp that they can hear and locate every rustle of a roosting bird in a bush, every squeak of a mouse in a yard, every wriggle of a worm under the lawn.

On the whole, they sit on their perch and wait for their prey to stir. If they drop down rapidly and silently on a mouse, they spread their wings to trap it as they strike it. They will dive into a bush to pick up a sleepy blackbird, or stand motionless on the grass like that blackbird, listening for the worms.

Freezing nights with still air give them no trouble. It is only on windy nights that they find life difficult, since the sound of the wind makes it harder for them to hear. However, they can be very noisy themselves when necessary, hooting loudly if they detect another tawny threatening to invade their territory.

Barn owls are equally at home in the dark, but they hunt mainly on the wing, and usually set out in the evening and go on into the dawn. One sometimes sees their wobbly, white shapes in the dusk as they pass with wavering wing strokes along a hedge, their face turned to the ground.

Little owls are often seen in broad daylight, sitting on a field gate and looking for beetles. When they are agitated, they bob up and down furiously. But they too are mainly nocturnal birds, just as well equipped as the other owls to hunt in the dark.

Long-eared owls are more rarely seen. In winter, they roost in daytime in thick bushes, and I have watched a pair of them sitting in the depths of a hawthorn on an island on a lake, almost invisible except for their orange eyes in their cat-like faces. Short-eared owls are, by contrast, out and about for most of the day over moors and marshes, wheeling and gliding with their wings held in a V-shape.

Meanwhile, what about the scops owl that astounded the Oxfordshire village of Thrupp for two summers with its night-time song? Or the pair of eagle owls that nested at Dunsop Bridge in the Lancashire fells? Let us hope that these rarities are skulking somewhere in the damp fields.

December

A long Scottish coasts on winter nights, a mysterious music can sometimes be heard coming from far out at sea. The Scots liken it to bagpipe music, other people call it yodelling. The music-makers are long-tailed ducks that have come down from their breeding pools on the treeless plains of the tundra. They often stay well out to sea when they are diving to find food on the seabed, because they can go down to a depth of fifty-five metres. This gives them a distinct advantage over other sea duck. However, they are not shy birds, and one frequently sees them quite close to the shore. I have watched them from the top of an Edinburgh bus as it passed by the water at Musselburgh.

They are easy to recognise. The drakes have long, curly tails, and in winter are mostly black and white, with a shapeless dark patch on the cheek that looks like a bad bruise. From the long tails they have got the name 'sea pheasant'. The females are more brown and white, but they too have the conspicuous cheek patch. Both have a little, round head with a steep forehead.

Long-Tailed Duck

It is the drakes that make the musical calls, and they can be heard constantly both by day and by night, but of course the calls are more noticeable in the dark. A strange, old Scottish name for them was 'col-candle-wick', which is an imitation of the call, while a nineteenth-century American name for them was 'old squaws', because they always seemed to be chattering away telling tales.

They are particularly noisy when they are courting, which they have already started doing, even in the days before midwinter. A group of drakes swims around a female, each of them bowing deeply to her and lifting its tail up high. They hold themselves up in this position for a few moments by kicking the water with their feet. By quite early in the new year they will have paired up.

They are still coming in from the north, and the largest assemblies are found in the Moray Firth. They are less common on the west side of Scotland, but they can be quite common on the northeast coast of England. Odd individuals can turn up anywhere along the coast, and some appear inland. I was amazed to see one a few years ago on a small lake in the Lea Valley just north of London, swimming about contentedly among tufted ducks.

Pink-footed geese have become important wintering birds in Britain. Fifty years ago about 10,000 of them would come each year from Iceland and Greenland; now about 300,000 arrive and most of them are already here.

Vast flocks fill the fields in eastern Scotland and rise with a thunder of wings when they are disturbed. Thousands roost on the Wash and go into the fields of sugar-beet in Norfolk and Lincolnshire. They are also found in great numbers round the Solway Firth. They sometimes feed in the fields by moonlight. Around Formby in Lancashire, where farmland is close to the town, they have been found feeding in fields illuminated by the street lights.

These relatively small geese are grazing birds, pinkish-grey with a dark-brown head. I have watched them come in at dawn from the Wash at Snettisham in Norfolk, flock after flock passing overhead with their ringing cries. If you put your hands behind your ears as a flock approaches, the sound is almost deafening. When they land in the fields, they often sideslip and come crashing down. But the snow has made life difficult for them. In some parts of Norfolk it has been fairly thin and the geese have been able to get at the sugar-beet leavings that they love to eat. But many have had to go to the fields of long, rough grass above the snow and eat that. Many have also gone to the estuaries, where they have eaten the plants of the saltmarshes, such as the prickly saltwort and the purplish suaeda.

Pink-Footed Goose

The Scottish geese have had a harder time and many have gone to the coast. People in Edinburgh and the surrounding country have become accustomed to the sight of V- or W-shaped skeins of pink-foots heading east. When the weather eased a bit, they started to return and fly in the opposite direction. But they have a good deal of winter to get through yet. The Arctic stays cold for a long time and they will not want to leave us for their breeding sites before the beginning of April.

There is a new bird on the scene. This is the penduline tit, a little bird of the willows and reed beds of Eastern Europe that has slowly been extending its range westward. It is rather like a tiny red-backed shrike, with a pale body, a reddish back and a black mask round its eyes. It also has a longish tail, which it uses a lot as it twists and turns through the reeds.

In recent years it has been found breeding as far west as Belgium, and there is now a large population in Spain. The first one known to have been seen in Britain was in 1966, and since 1986 some of them have been seen here every year. There have been quite frequent records at Rainham Marshes, east of London.

I have seen them in a swamp beside the Vistula where

this great river flows through the outskirts of Warsaw. I have also seen their nests there, and these are a remarkable sight. The ones I saw were hanging, characteristically, from the end of willow twigs overhanging a reed bed. They are domed nests with a little spout like a handle high up at the side, through which the birds come and go. They are woven out of fibrous plants such as nettles, and lined with the soft seeds from crumbling bulrush heads. It is said they were once used as slippers by poor peasants.

The breeding birds themselves also live a remarkable life. After the male has paired, he leaves his mate and starts building nests in the hope of attracting other females. He may end up with several families, but he sometimes returns to his first mate and helps her with hers. However, some females also have a riotous life, finding several partners and laying eggs for all of them. In these circumstances, the males find themselves looking after the families.

The incubating birds get some company as others come and look at them through the spout. The young birds do not seem to suffer from what seems like a rather chancy upbringing.

Penduline tits also feed in the reed beds, swaying on the stems as they pick off the seeds. I saw a bird doing this in a reed bed in Essex only last week, and I looked very carefully at it, but it proved to be a reed bunting.

However, the chances of seeing one are evidently increasing. And one day soon there may be heard a shout of joy as someone sees the first British nest hanging among the willow leaves.

Last weekend I was watching two pairs of goldeneyes diving on a large lake. These handsome ducks, which come here for the winter from Finland and Russia, really do have golden eyes, sharp and glittering. But the drakes, which have dark-green heads, also have a round, white spot on their cheek. This makes it easy to identify them, but diverts attention from their eyes – and I think that some people believe that these white marks actually are the golden eyes. They also have a fascinating head shape, with a long, steep forehead and a peaked top. If ever a bird looked like an intellectual, it is this one.

The females also have golden eyes, in a blackish-brown head, but it was this sloping forehead that picked them out for me among the great flotilla of tufted ducks and coots swimming around them.

The other thing that told me these four birds were goldeneyes was that they were hardly ever there. They were such enthusiastic divers that the moment you saw one of them it was gone, throwing up its tail and vanishing with scarcely a ripple. It was on the bottom of the lake, trawling with its beak for such food as mayfly larvae and little fish. Goldeneyes can stay underwater for up to a half a minute. Invisible bird equals goldeneye.

Formerly they were known only as winter visitors to Britain. Strangely for a duck, they nest in trees. In Russia, in the summer, they often use the holes made by black woodpeckers, a bird that has never been seen in this country.

However, in 1970, a pair nested in Scotland, in a tree hole in the Spey Valley. This inspired bird enthusiasts to put up some specially designed nest boxes there. The goldeneyes took to them and there are now about 200 pairs nesting there each summer, though they have never gone far from Speyside.

Nowadays, on the lochs there in spring, the ringing whistles of the courting goldeneyes can be heard half a mile away. They are well worth a visit, especially as Speyside is also the best place to go to see nesting ospreys and crested tits, which are little black-and-white relatives of the blue tit, found in Britain only in the Highland pine forests.

Great northern divers are large, handsome birds that appear around our shores in winter. They generally fish far out to sea, often as much as five or six miles from the coast. But shoals of herring bring them closer to land, and so do strong west winds over the Atlantic. Many of them died in the oil spills off the Scilly Isles in the *Torrey Canyon* oil tanker disaster in March 1967.

At this time of year, there is often a scattering of them on inland lakes and reservoirs. They have been seen out on Staines reservoir in Surrey, the Queen Mother Reservoir in Berkshire, Grafham Water in Cambridgeshire and West Kirby Marine Lake in Cheshire.

Recently a driver found one lying on the Ashford ring road in Kent. He thought at first it was a black bin liner, but then he saw it lift its head, so he took it to the RSPCA at Mallydams Wood. When it was taken out of the boot of the car it stabbed with its beak at everything, but the RSPCA put it on a pool to rest, and four hours later they were able to release it unharmed.

When great northern divers are swimming low in the water you might mistake them for a cormorant – of which there are now plenty inland in winter. But the cormorant has a much longer neck, and also its curious long, hooked beak, lifted in the air, is quite different from the diver's ferocious dagger, which is held horizontally.

In summer, great northern divers are spectacular birds, with a beautifully chequered back, a black head with a green sheen, and a white collar. In winter their back is dark grey with a faintly scalloped pattern, and there is still a trace of the collar on their neck. They are duller, but still rather fine.

The birds seen here have come from Iceland and Greenland, and some from the Canadian lakes. They make their nests of vegetation at the water's edge, and when the young are small they ride on their parents' backs. Very rarely a pair has nested in northern Scotland, and a few non-breeding birds linger here in summer. I have seen them resplendent in their breeding plumage off the Outer Hebrides, and on Islay I watched one diving in the Port Charlotte harbour while I was having breakfast in the hotel.

In North America they are called loons, and are famous for their wailing cries in summer which are like mad laughter and weeping. These cries have been used as a chilling soundtrack in many films, where they have not always been appropriate.

There are still wild turkeys in the world, though they are not in Turkey. They never were. The wild turkey is an American bird, and still roams the forests and swamps from Florida to Mexico. Our domestic turkeys are the direct descendants of these American turkeys, and resemble them in most respects. But why are they called turkeys?

The answer is this. They were first brought to Europe in the sixteenth century by the Spanish, who had discovered them in Mexico, but they were imported into England by the so-called Turkey merchants, or traders with the East. The Turkey merchants also brought in guinea fowl from Africa, and both birds were at first known as turkeys. The name stuck with the bird that eventually became our Christmas dinner.

Wild Turkey

In the US, of course, they are eaten at Thanksgiving. But these table birds are also farmed birds. Native turkeys are quite wild, shy birds. The males look like old Norfolk turkeys, brown or sometimes black, with reflections of bronze or green in their feathers. Like the farmyard birds, they have a bare head and neck with red wattles. They gobble loudly too.

The wild birds are not fat creatures waddling about with dislocated hips and too heavy to fly. They slip briskly through the undergrowth in search of fruit and insects, and fly up on to tree branches to roost. The males do not help with the bringing up of the young, but the females and their offspring form large wandering flocks after the breeding season.

Wild turkeys used to be found much further north than they are now. They were so familiar to Americans that Benjamin Franklin wanted the turkey to be the country's national bird. Their numbers declined not only because they were killed for food, but also because they were shot when they invaded cornfields to feed in the autumn.

Now they offer a rare delight to American birdwatchers who manage to spot them. However, in some places they have been reintroduced, and there are even some in California, where they were never known before.

Visiting the Netherlands for a few days last week, I had an unexpected pleasure when I was passing on the train through the countryside around Dordrecht. One after another I saw three hen harriers flapping and gliding over the dank fields.

They are handsome raptors, and look quite sinister as they fly slowly to and fro, quartering the ground, the feathers of their wing tips spread like daggers. They are quite common in the Dutch wetlands in winter, and Lelystad, the 'new town' of the polders, further north than Dordrecht, has even adopted them as its symbol. They are tamer up there, sitting on the tops of roadside trees, indifferent to the traffic.

A fair number of them also visit this country in the winter, and are seen over estuaries and marshes, especially in eastern England. The three birds I saw would probably have joined up in the evening, since they roost together in reed beds or in long, rough grass, going back alone to their hunting territories in the morning.

In summer four or five hundred pairs nest on the heather moors, mainly in Scotland, with a few in north-west England and Wales. Their aerial displays in spring are one of the glories of the moors. The male rises steeply into the sky and plummets down again, sometimes turning a somersault on the way. Or he circles wildly round the female in mid-air, while she turns momentarily on to her back.

The Royal Society for the Protection of Birds has put a lot of effort into protecting these fine birds, but many managers of grouse moors and gamekeepers regard them as a serious threat to the grouse, and harriers are still persecuted, generally illegally. Moor owners have themselves spent a lot of money in recent years on restoring the grouse moors, and plenty of other wildlife, including the harriers, have returned. But do the harriers reduce the grouse numbers?

Some years ago a Game and Wildlife Conservation Trust study was carried out on the Langholm estate in the Scottish Borders. Hen harriers were allowed to flourish unchecked, and the grouse population virtually collapsed. The RSPB is not very much worried by this study. It still takes the view that proper management of the moors, with plenty of other birds and small animals for the harriers to feed on, will allow the harriers and grouse to live side by side.

A new visitor to some garden feeders in the last year or two has been the lesser redpoll. Like goldfinches, it seems to favour nyjer seeds, and it has been a pleasant surprise. However, it is not a very common bird these days. In the late 1960s and early 1970s it became quite abundant and its harsh twitter was heard overhead almost everywhere.

This was probably due to the extensive planting of conifers at that time. The young trees provided perfect nesting places for this bird that likes to build in thick bushes. Now the trees have grown tall, and are no longer a natural breeding place for them. Nor are there many replacements, for the fashion for creating new conifer plantations has faded.

They are very attractive, lively birds, like small linnets. They have a red forehead and a small, black bib, and the males have a red breast in spring and summer. Like many birds, they have dull tips to their colourful feathers when they first come out of the autumn moult, but these tips wear away to reveal the colour as winter proceeds.

They have always been commonest in summer in Scotland and the north of England, but many of them come south after they have finished nesting, some going abroad, some staying in southern England. Their winter food is mainly alder and birch seeds, and those are the trees in which to look for them. They flock into the crown of the tree, and swing upside down on the twigs to get at the seeds. Siskins and goldfinches also feed in alders and birches, and one can sometimes see all three species together.

The lesser redpoll has lost its name and gained it again in recent years. There is a larger, paler redpoll in Scandinavia and places further east, and for a while this bird and our bird were joined together as a single species under the name 'common redpoll' or just 'redpoll'. Now this paler bird has been recognised as a full species with the name either of 'common redpoll' or 'mealy redpoll', and our bird has got the name 'lesser redpoll' back again.

Quite a few of these common or mealy redpolls come here in winter. But there is an even larger and whiter redpoll that lives further east, called the Arctic redpoll – and that too can turn up here as a rare visitor. Beware the taxonomists – they are a restless tribe, and I should not be surprised to see them change all these names and distinctions again.

Last week, when it was already chilly but just before winter struck hard, I saw a jewelled spectacle on a lake in Essex. It was a flock of about 450 teal, spread out all over the water, with the midday sun behind me shining straight on them. There was a little thin, floating ice at one end of the lake, but not enough to trouble them.

Drake teal are astonishingly beautiful birds. They have a reddish-chestnut head with a glittering green, comma-shaped mark on either side of it. In front of their tail they have a golden-yellow patch. They also have a bright green square on their wing, which is often invisible when they are swimming, but which every moment flashed out on one bird's wing or another. The body is a finely speckled grey. The female is a mottled brown, but she, too, has the green wing-patch. To see a lake almost covered with these ducks, all shining in the sun, was a remarkable experience.

There was also a soft music coming from the water. The drakes often whistle quietly as they swim, and many of these drakes were doing so today.

The teal were practically the only birds on the lake, apart from a few coot nodding their way round it. But then I saw two drake pintail swimming about among the teal in a lordly fashion. These are also handsome birds. They have a fairly long neck, with a mainly chocolate-coloured head and a delicate, vertical white line behind it. At the other end they have a sharply pointed tail with a yellow patch, like the teal's, in front of it. A moment later I noticed two brown-headed females swimming patiently a little way behind them.

Now the lake is frozen solid. Teal feed mainly on seeds floating in the water and they move on swiftly when they cannot get at them. The pintail may have gone down to the sea. The teal, though, are probably basking already on a lake in the south of France or in Spain. They are fast flyers and have far less trouble than humans in making their getaway.

Index